PIONEERS OF THE OLD SOUTH

TEXTBOOK EDITION

∴

THE YALE CHRONICLES
OF AMERICA SERIES
ALLEN JOHNSON
EDITOR

GERHARD R. LOMER
CHARLES W. JEFFERYS
ASSISTANT EDITORS

PIONEERS
OF THE OLD SOUTH

A CHRONICLE OF ENGLISH
COLONIAL BEGINNINGS
BY MARY JOHNSTON

TORONTO: GLASGOW, BROOK & CO.
NEW YORK: UNITED STATES PUBLISHERS
ASSOCIATION, INC.

CONTENTS

PIONEERS OF THE OLD SOUTH

∴

CHAPTER I

THE THREE SHIPS SAIL

ELIZABETH of England died in 1603. There came to the English throne James Stuart, King of Scotland, King now of England and Scotland. In 1604 a treaty of peace ended the long war with Spain. Gone was the sixteenth century; here, though in childhood, was the seventeenth century.

Now that the wars were over, old colonization schemes were revived in the English mind. Of the motives which in the first instance had prompted these schemes, some with the passing of time had become weaker, some remained quite as strong as before. Most Englishmen and women knew now that Spain had clay feet; and that Rome, though she might threaten, could not always perform what she threatened. To abase the pride of Spain, to make harbors of refuge for the angel of the Reformation — these wishes, though they had not vanished, though no man could know how long the peace with Spain would last, were less fervid than they had been in the days of Drake. But the old desire for trade remained as strong as ever. It would be a great boon to have English markets in the New World, as well as in the Old, to which merchants might send their wares and from which might be drawn in bulk the raw stuffs that were needed at home. The idea of a surplus population persisted; England of five million souls still thought that she was crowded and that it would be well to have a land of younger sons, a land of promise for all not abundantly provided for at home. It were surely well, for mere pride's sake, to have due lot and part in the great New World! And wealth like that which Spain had found was a dazzle and a lure. "Why, man, all their dripping-pans are pure gold, and all the chains with which they chain up their streets are massy gold; all the prisoners they take are fettered in gold; and for rubies and diamonds they go forth on holidays and gather 'em by the seashore!" So the comedy of *Eastward Ho!* seen on the London stage in 1605 — "Eastward Ho!" because yet they thought of America as on the road around to China.

In this year Captain George Weymouth sailed across the sea and spent a summer month in North Virginia — later, New England. Weymouth had powerful backers, and with him sailed old adventurers who had been with Raleigh. Coming home to England with five Indians in his company, Weymouth and his voyage gave to public interest the needed fillip towards action. Here was the peace with Spain, and here was the new interest in Virginia. "Go to!" said Mother England. "It is time to place our children in the world!"

The old adventurers of the day of Sir Humphrey Gilbert had acted as individuals. Soon was to come in the idea of coöperative action — the idea of the joint-stock company, acting under the open permission of the Crown, attended by the interest and favor of numbers of the people, and giving to private initiative and personal ambition a public tone. Some men of foresight would have had Crown and Country themselves the adventurers, superseding any smaller bodies. But for the moment the fortunes of Virginia were furthered by a group within the great group, by a joint-stock company, **a** corporation.

In 1600 had come into being the East India Company, prototype of many companies to follow. Now, six years later, there arose under one royal charter two companies, generally known as the London and the Plymouth. The first colony planted by the latter was short-lived. Its letters patent were for North Virginia. Two ships, the *Mary and John* and the *Gift of God*, sailed with over a hundred settlers. These men, reaching the coast of what is now Maine, built a fort and a church on the banks of the Kennebec. Then followed the usual miseries typical of colonial venture — sickness, starvation, and a freezing winter. With the return of summer the enterprise was abandoned. The foundation of New England was delayed awhile, her Pilgrims yet in England, though meditating that first remove to Holland, her *Mayflower* only a ship of London port, staunch, but with no fame above another.

The London Company, soon to become the Virginia Company, therefore engages our attention. The charter recites that Sir Thomas Gates and Sir George Somers, Knights, Richard Hakluyt, clerk, Prebendary of Westminster, Edward-

Maria Wingfield, and other knights, gentlemen, merchants, and adventurers, wish "to make habitation, plantation, and to deduce a colony of sundry of our people into that part of America commonly called Virginia." It covenants with them and gives them for a heritage all America between the thirty-fourth and the forty-first parallels of latitude.

The thirty-fourth parallel passes through the middle of what is now South Carolina; the forty-first grazes New York, crosses the northern tip of New Jersey, divides Pennsylvania, and so westward across to that Pacific or South Sea that the age thought so near to the Atlantic. All England might have been placed many times over in what was given to those knights, gentlemen, merchants, and others.

The King's charter created a great Council of Virginia, sitting in London, governing from overhead. In the new land itself there should exist a second and lesser council. The two councils had authority within the range of Virginian matters, but the Crown retained the power of veto. The Council in Virginia might coin money for trade with the Indians, expel invaders, import settlers, punish ill-doers, levy and collect taxes — should have, in short, dignity and power enough for any colony. Likewise, acting for the whole, it might give and take orders "to dig, mine and search for all manner of mines of gold, silver and copper . . . to have and enjoy . . . yielding to us, our heirs and successors, the fifth part only of all the same gold and silver, and the fifteenth part of all the same copper."

Now are we ready — it being Christmas-tide of the year 1606 — to go to Virginia. Riding on the Thames, before Blackwall, are three ships, small enough in all conscience' sake, the *Susan Constant*, the *Goodspeed*, and the *Discovery*. The Admiral of this fleet is Christopher Newport, an old seaman of Raleigh's. Bartholomew Gosnold captains the *Goodspeed*, and John Ratcliffe the *Discovery*. The three ships have aboard their crews and one hundred and twenty colonists, all men. The Council in Virginia is on board — but it does not yet know itself as such, for the names of its members have been deposited by the superior home council in a sealed box, to be opened only on Virginia soil.

The colonists have their paper of instructions. They shall find out a safe port in the entrance of a navigable river. They shall be prepared against surprise and attack. They shall observe "whether the river on which you plant doth spring out of mountains or out of lakes. If it be out of any lake the passage to the other sea will be the more easy, and like enough . . . you shall find some spring which runs the contrary way toward the East India sea." They must avoid giving offense to the "naturals" — must choose a healthful place for their houses — must guard their shipping. They are to set down in black and white for the information of the Council at home all such matters as directions and distances, the nature of soils and forests and the various commodities that they may find. And no man is to return from Virginia without leave from the Council, and none is to write home any discouraging letter. The instructions end, "Lastly and chiefly, the way to prosper and to achieve good success is to make yourselves all of one mind for the good of your country and your own, and to serve and fear God, the Giver of all Goodness, for every plantation which our Heavenly Father hath not planted shall be rooted out."

Nor did they lack verses to go by, as their enterprise itself did not lack poetry. Michael Drayton wrote for them:—

PIONEERS OF THE OLD SOUTH

Britons, you stay too long,
Quickly aboard bestow you,
 And with a merry gale,
 Swell your stretched sail,
With vows as strong
As the winds that blow you.

Your course securely steer,
West and by South forth keep;
 Rocks, lee shores nor shoals,
 Where Eolus scowls,
You need not fear,
So absolute the deep.

And cheerfully at sea
Success you still entice,
 To get the pearl and gold,
 And ours to hold
VIRGINIA,
Earth's only paradise! . . .

And in regions far
Such heroes bring ye forth
 As those from whom we came;
 And plant our name
Under that star
Not known unto our north.

See the parting upon Thames's side, Englishmen going, English kindred, friends, and neighbors
calling farewell, waving hat and scarf, standing
bare-headed in the gray winter weather! To Vir-

ginia — they are going to Virginia! The sails are made upon the *Susan Constant*, the *Goodspeed*, and the *Discovery*. The last wherry carries aboard the last adventurer. The anchors are weighed. Down the river the wind bears the ships toward the sea. Weather turning against them, they taste long delay in the Downs, but at last are forth upon the Atlantic. Hourly the distance grows between London town and the out-going folk, between English shores and where the surf breaks on the pale Virginian beaches. Far away — far away and long ago — yet the unseen, actual cables hold, and yesterday and today stand embraced, the lips of the Thames meet the lips of the James, and the breath of England mingles with the breath of America.

CHAPTER II

THE ADVENTURERS

What was this Virginia to which they were bound? In the sixteenth and early seventeenth centuries the name stood for a huge stretch of littoral, running southward from lands of long winters and fur-bearing animals to lands of the canebrake, the fig, the magnolia, the chameleon, and the mocking-bird. The world had been circumnavigated; Drake had passed up the western coast — and yet cartographers, the learned, and those who took the word from the learned, strangely visualized the North American mainland as narrow indeed. Apparently they conceived it as a kind of extended Central America. The huge rivers puzzled them. There existed a notion that these might be estuaries, curling and curving through the land from sea to sea. India — Cathay — spices and wonders and Orient wealth — lay beyond the South Sea, and the South Sea was but a few days' march from

Hatteras or Chesapeake. The Virginia familiar to the mind of the time lay extended, and she was very slender. Her right hand touched the eastern ocean, and her left hand touched the western.

Contact and experience soon modified this general notion. Wider knowledge, political and economic considerations, practical reasons of all kinds, drew a different physical form for old Virginia. Before the seventeenth century had passed away, they had given to her northern end a baptism of other names. To the south she was lopped to make the Carolinas. Only to the west, for a long time, she seemed to grow, while like a mirage the South Sea and Cathay receded into the distance.

This narrative, moving with the three ships from England, and through a time span of less than a hundred and fifty years, deals with a region of the western hemisphere a thousand miles in length, several hundred in breadth, stretching from the Florida line to the northern edge of Chesapeake Bay, and from the Atlantic to the Appalachians. Out of this Virginia there grow in succession the ancient colonies and the modern States of Virginia, Maryland, South and North Carolina, and Georgia.

But for many a year Virginia itself was the only

settlement and the only name. This Virginia was a country favored by nature. Neither too hot nor too cold, it was rich-soiled and capable of every temperate growth in its sunniest aspect. Great rivers drained it, flowing into a great bay, almost a sea, many-armed as Briareus, affording safe and sheltered harbors. Slowly, with beauty, the land mounted to the west. The sun set behind wooded mountains, long wave-lines raised far back in geologic time. The valleys were many and beautiful, watered by sliding streams. Back to the east again, below the rolling land, were found the shimmering levels, the jewel-green marshes, the wide, slow waters, and at last upon the Atlantic shore the thunder of the rainbow-tinted surf. Various and pleasing was the country. Springs and autumns were long and balmy, the sun shone bright, there was much blue sky, a rich flora and fauna. There were mineral wealth and water power, and breadth and depth for agriculture. Such was the Virginia between the Potomac and the Dan, the Chesapeake and the Alleghanies.

This, and not the gold-bedight slim neighbor of Cathay, was now the lure of the *Susan Constant,* the *Goodspeed,* and the *Discovery.* But those aboard, obsessed by Spanish America, imperfectly knowing the features and distances of the orb, yet clung to their first vision. But they knew there would be forest and Indians. Tales enough had been told of both!

What has to be imaged is a forest the size of Virginia. Here and there, chiefly upon river banks, show small Indian clearings. Here and there are natural meadows, and toward the salt water great marshes, the home of waterfowl. But all these are little or naught in the whole, faint adornments sewed upon a shaggy garment, green in summer, flame-hued in autumn, brown in winter, green and flower-colored in the spring. Nor was the forest to any appreciable extent like much Virginian forest of today, second growth, invaded, hewed down, and renewed, to hear again the sound of the axe, set afire by a thousand accidents, burning upon its own funeral pyres, all its primeval glory withered. The forest of old Virginia was jocund and powerful, eternally young and eternally old. The forest was Despot in the land — was Emperor and Pope.

With the forest went the Indian. They had a pact together. The Indians hacked out space for their villages of twenty or thirty huts, their maize and bean fields and tobacco patches. They took

saplings for poles and bark to cover the huts and
wood for fires. The forest gave canoe and bow
and arrow, household bowls and platters, the sides
of the drum that was beaten at feasts. It furnished trees serviceable for shelter when the foe
was stalked. It was their wall and roof, their habitat. It was one of the Four Friends of the Indian
— the Ground, the Waters, the Sky, the Forest.
The forest was everywhere, and the Indians
dwelled in the forest. Not unnaturally they held
that this world was theirs.

Upon the three ships, sailing, sailing, moved a
few men who could speak with authority of the
forest and of Indians. Christopher Newport was
upon his first voyage to Virginia, but he knew the
Indies and the South American coast. He had
sailed and had fought under Francis Drake. And
Bartholomew Gosnold had explored both for himself and for Raleigh. These two could tell others
what to look for. In their company there was also
John Smith. This gentleman, it is true, had not
wandered, fought, and companioned with romance
in America, but he had done so everywhere else.
He had as yet no experience with Indians, but
he could conceive that rough experiences were
rough experiences, whether in Europe, Asia, Africa,

or America. And as he knew there was a family likeness among dangerous happenings, so also he found one among remedies, and he had a bag full of stories of strange happenings and how they should be met.

They were going the old, long West Indies sea road. There was time enough for talking, wondering, considering the past, fantastically building up the future. Meeting in the ships' cabins over ale tankards, pacing up and down the small high-raised poop-decks, leaning idle over the side, watching the swirling dark-blue waters or the stars of night, lying idle upon the deck, propped by the mast while the trade-winds blew and up beyond sail and rigging curved the sky — they had time enough indeed to plan for marvels! If they could have seen ahead, what pictures of things to come they might have beheld rising, falling, melting one into another!

Certain of the men upon the *Susan Constant,* the *Goodspeed,* and the *Discovery* stand out clearly, etched against the sky.

Christopher Newport might be forty years old. He had been of Raleigh's captains and was chosen, a very young man, to bring to England from the Indies the captured great carrack, *Madre de Dios,* laden with fabulous treasure. In all, Newport was destined to make five voyages to Virginia, carrying supply and aid. After that, he would pass into the service of the East India Company, know India, Java, and the Persian Gulf; would be praised by that great company for sagacity, energy, and good care of his men. Ten years' time from this first Virginia voyage, and he would die upon his ship, the *Hope*, before Bantam in Java.

Bartholomew Gosnold, the captain of the *Goodspeed*, had sailed with thirty others, five years before, from Dartmouth in a bark named the *Concord*. He had not made the usual long sweep southward into tropic waters, there to turn and come northward, but had gone, arrow-straight, across the north Atlantic — one of the first English sailors to make the direct passage and save many a weary sea league. Gosnold and his men had seen Cape Ann and Cape Cod, and had built upon Cuttyhunk, among the Elizabeth Islands, a little fort thatched with rushes. Then, hardships thronging and quarrels developing, they had filled their ship with sassafras and cedar and sailed for home over the summer Atlantic, reaching England, with "not one cake of bread" left but only "a little vinegar." Gosnold, guiding the *Goodspeed*, is now making his last voyage, for he is to die in Virginia within the year.

George Percy, brother of the Earl of Northumberland, has fought bravely in the Low Countries. He is to stay five years in Virginia, to serve there a short time as Governor, and then, returning to England, is to write *A Trewe Relacyion*, in which he begs to differ from John Smith's *Generall Historie*. Finally he goes again to the wars in the Low Countries, serves with distinction, and dies, unmarried, at the age of fifty-two. His portrait shows a long, rather melancholy face, set between a lace collar and thick, dark hair.

A Queen and a Cardinal — Mary Tudor and Reginald Pole — had stood sponsors for the father of Edward-Maria Wingfield. This man, of an ancient and honorable stock, was older than most of his fellow adventurers to Virginia. He had fought in Ireland, fought in the Low Countries, had been a prisoner of war. Now he was presently to become "the first president of the first council in the first English colony in America." And then, miseries increasing and wretched men being quick to impute evil, it was to be held with other assertions against him that he was of a Catholic family, that he traveled without a Bible, and probably meant to betray Virginia to the Spaniard. He was to be deposed from his presidency, return to England, and there write a vindication. "I never turned my face from daunger, or hidd my handes from labour; so watchful a sentinel stood myself to myself." With John Smith he had a bitter quarrel.

Upon the *Discovery* is one who signed himself "John Radclyffe, comenly called," and who is named in the London Company's list as "Captain John Sicklemore, *alias* Ratcliffe." He will have a short and stormy Virginian life, and in two years be done to death by Indians. John Smith quarreled with him also. "A poor counterfeited Imposture!" said Smith. Gabriel Archer is a lawyer, and first secretary or recorder of the colony. Short, too, is his life. His name lives in Archer's Hope on the James River in Virginia. John Smith will have none of him! George Kendall's life is more nearly spun than Ratcliffe's or Archer's. He will be shot for treason and rebellion. Robert Hunt is the chaplain. Besides those whom the time dubbed "gentlemen," there are upon the three ships English sailors, English laborers, six carpenters, two bricklayers, a blacksmith, a tailor, a barber, a drummer, other craftsmen, and nondescripts. Up and down and to and fro they pass in their narrow quarters, microscopic upon the bosom of the ocean.

John Smith looms large among them. John Smith has a mantle of marvelous adventure. It seems that he began to make it when he was a boy, and for many years worked upon it steadily until it was stiff as cloth of gold and voluminous as a puffed-out summer cloud. Some think that much of it was such stuff as dreams are made of. Probably some breadths were the fabric of vision. Still it seems certain that he did have some kind of an extraordinary coat or mantle. The adventures which he relates of himself are those of a paladin. Born in 1579 or 1580, he was at this time still a young man. But already he had fought in France and in the Netherlands, and in Transylvania against the Turks. He had known sea-fights and shipwrecks and had journeyed, with adventures galore, in Italy. Before Regall, in Transylvania, ne had challenged three Turks in succession, unhorsed them, and cut off their heads, for which doughty deed Sigismund, a Prince of Transylvania, had given him a coat of arms showing three Turks' heads in a shield. Later he had been taken in battle and sold into slavery, whereupon a Turkish lady, his master's sister, had looked upon him with favor. But at last he slew the Turk and escaped, and after wandering many days in misery came into Russia. "Here, too, I found, as I have always done when in misfortune, kindly help from a woman." He wandered on into Germany and thence into France and Spain. Hearing of wars in Barbary, he crossed from Gibraltar. Here he met the captain of a French man-of-war. One day while he was with this man there arose a great storm which drove the ship out to sea. They went before the wind to the Canaries, and there put themselves to rights and began to chase Spanish barks. Presently they had a great fight with two Spanish men-of-war, in which the French ship and Smith came off victors. Returning to Morocco, Smith bade the French captain good-bye and took ship for England, and so reached home in 1604. Here he sought the company of like-minded men, and so came upon those who had been to the New World — "and all their talk was of its wonders." So Smith joined the Virginia undertaking, and so we find him headed toward new adventures in the western world.

On sailed the three ships — little ships — sailing-ships with a long way to go.

The twelfth day of February at night we saw a blaz-
ing starre and presently a storme. . . . The three and
twentieth day [of March] we fell with the Iland of
Mattanenio in the West Indies. The foure and twentieth day we anchored at Dominico, within fourteene
degrees of the Line, a very faire Iland, full of sweet and
good smells, inhabited by many Savage Indians. . . .
The six and twentieth day we had sight of Marigalanta,
and the next day wee sailed with a slacke sail alongst
the Ile of Guadalupa. . . . We sailed by many Ilands,
as Mounserot and an Iland called Saint Christopher,
both uninhabited; about two a clocke in the afternoone
wee anchored at the Ile of Mevis. There the Captaine
landed all his men. . . . We incamped ourselves on
this Ile six days. . . . The tenth day [April] we set
saile and disimboged out of the West Indies and bare
our course Northerly. . . . The six and twentieth day
of Aprill, about foure a clocke in the morning, wee de-
scried the Land of Virginia.[1]

During the long months of this voyage, cramped
in the three ships, these men, most of them young
and of the hot-blooded, physically adventurous
sort, had time to develop strong likings and dis-
likings. The hundred and twenty split into opposed camps. The several groups nursed all
manner of jealousies. Accusations flew between
like shuttlecocks. The sealed box that they carried

[1] Percy's *Discourse* in *Purchas, His Pilgrims*, vol. IV. p. 1684
Also given in Brown's *Genesis of the United States*. vol. I. p. 152.

proved a manner of Até's apple. All knew that
seven on board were councilors and rulers, with
one of the number President, but they knew not
which were the seven. Smith says that this uncertainty wrought much mischief, each man of
note suggesting to himself, "I shall be President
— or, at least, Councilor!" The ships became
cursed with a pest of factions. A prime quarrel
arose between John Smith and Edward-Maria
Wingfield, two whose temperaments seem to have
been poles apart. There arose a "scandalous
report" that Smith meant to reach Virginia only
to usurp the Government, murder the Council,
and proclaim himself King. The bickering deepened into forthright quarrel, with at last the
expected explosion. Smith was arrested, was put
in irons, and first saw Virginia as a prisoner.

On the twenty-sixth day of April, 1607, the
Susan Constant, the *Goodspeed*, and the *Discovery*
entered Chesapeake Bay. They came in between
two capes, and one they named Cape Henry after
the then Prince of Wales, and the other Cape
Charles for that brother of short-lived Henry who
was to become Charles the First. By Cape Henry
they anchored, and numbers from the ships went
ashore. "But," says George Percy's *Discourse,*

"we could find nothing worth the speaking of, but faire meadows and goodly tall Trees, with such Fresh-waters running through the woods as I was almost ravished at the first sight thereof. At night, when wee were going aboard, there came the Savages creeping upon all foure from the Hills like Beares, with their Bowes in their mouths, charged us very desperately in the faces, hurt Captaine Gabriel Archer in both his hands, and a sayler in two places of the body very dangerous. After they had spent their Arrowes and felt the sharpnesse of our shot, they retired into the Woods with a great noise, and so left us."

That very night, by the ships' lanterns, Newport, Gosnold, and Ratcliffe opened the sealed box. The names of the councilors were found to be Christopher Newport, Bartholomew Gosnold, John Ratcliffe, Edward-Maria Wingfield, John Martin, John Smith, and George Kendall, with Gabriel Archer for recorder. From its own number, at the first convenient time, this Council was to choose its President. All this was now declared and published to all the company upon the ships. John Smith was given his freedom but was not yet allowed place in the Council. So closed an exciting day.

In the morning they pressed in parties yet further into the land, but met no Indians — only came to a place where these savages had been roasting oysters. The next day saw further exploring. "We marched some three or foure miles further into the Woods where we saw great smoakes of fire. Wee marched to those smoakes and found that the Savages had beene there burning downe the grasse. . . . We passed through excellent ground full of Flowers of divers kinds and colours, and as goodly trees as I have seene, as cedar, cipresse and other kindes; going a little further we came into a little plat of ground full of fine and beautifull strawberries, foure times bigger and better than ours in England. All this march we could neither see Savage nor Towne."[1]

The ships now stood into those waters which we call Hampton Roads. Finding a good channel and taking heart therefrom, they named a horn of land Point Comfort. Now we call it Old Point Comfort. Presently they began to go up a great river which they christened the James. To English eyes it was a river hugely wide. They went slowly, with pauses and waitings and adventures. They consulted their paper of instructions; they

[1] Percy's *Discourse.*

scanned the shore for good places for their fort, for their town. It was May, and all the rich banks were in bloom. It seemed a sweet-scented world of promise. They saw Indians, but had with these no untoward encounters. Upon the twelfth of May they came to a point of land which they named Archer's Hope. Landing here, they saw "many squirels, conies, Black Birds with crimson wings, and divers other Fowles and Birds of divers and sundrie colours of crimson, watchet, Yellow, Greene, Murry, and of divers other hewes natur-ally without any art using . . . store of Turkie nests and many Egges." They liked this place, but for shoal water the ships could not come near to land. So on they went, eight miles up the river.

Here, upon the north side, thirty-odd miles from the mouth, they came to a certain peninsula, an island at high water. Two or three miles long, less than a mile and a half in breadth, at its widest place composed of marsh and woodland, it ran into the river, into six fathom water, where the ships might be moored to the trees. It was this convenient deep water that determined matters. Here came to anchor the *Susan Constant*, the *Good-speed*, and the *Discovery*. Here the colonists went ashore. Here the members of the Council were

sworn, and for first President was chosen Edward
Maria Wingfield. Here, the first roaming and excitement abated, they began to unlade the ships,
and to build the fort and also booths for their
present sleeping. A church, too, they must have
at once, and forthwith made it with a stretched
sail for roof and a board between two trees whereon to rest Bible and Book of Prayer. Here, for
the first time in all this wilderness, rang English
axe in American forest, here was English law and
an English town, here sounded English speech.
Here was placed the germ of that physical, mental,
and spiritual power which is called the United
States of America.

CHAPTER III

IN historians' accounts of the first months at Jamestown, too much, perhaps, has been made of faction and quarrel. All this was there. Men set down in a wilderness, amid Virginian heat, men mostly young, of the active rather than the reflective type, men uncompanioned by women and children, men beset with dangers and sufferings that were soon to tax heavily their courage and patience — such men naturally quarreled and made up, quarreled again and again made up, darkly suspected each the other, as they darkly suspected the forest and the Indian; then, need of friendship dominating, embraced each the other, felt the fascination of the forest, and trusted the Indian. However much they suspected rebellion, treacheries, and desertions, they practiced fidelities, though to varying degrees, and there was in

each man's breast more or less of courage and
good intent.   They were prone to call one another
villain, but actual villainy — save as jealousy, suspicion, and hatred are villainy — seems rarely to
have been present. Even one who was judged
a villain and shot for his villainy seems hardly to
have deserved such fate. Jamestown peninsula
turned out to be feverous; fantastic hopes were
matched by strange fears; there were homesickness, incompatibilities, unfamiliar food and water
and air, class differences in small space, some
petty tyrannies, and very certain dangers. The
worst summer heat was not yet, and the fort was
building. Trees must be felled, cabins raised, a
field cleared for planting, fishing and hunting
carried on. And some lading, some first fruits,
must go back in the ships. No gold or rubies being
as yet found, they would send instead cedar and
sassafras — hard work enough, there at Jamestown, in the Virginian low-country, with May
warm as northern midsummer, and all the air
charged with vapor from the heated river, with
exhalations from the rank forest, from the many
marshes.

"The first night of our landing, about midnight,"
says George Percy in his *Discourse*, "there came

some Savages sayling close to our quarter; presently there was an alarm given; upon that the savages ran away. . . . Not long after there came two Savages that seemed to be Commanders, bravely dressed, with Crownes of coloured haire upon their heads, which came as Messengers from the Werowance of Paspihe, telling us that their Werowance was comming and would be merry with us with a fat Deere. The eighteenth day the Werowance of Paspihe came himselfe to our quarter, with one hundred Savages armed which guarded him in very warlike manner with Bowes and Arrowes." Some misunderstanding arose. "The Werowance, [seeing] us take to our armes, went suddenly away with all his company in great anger." The nineteenth day Percy with several others going into the woods back of the peninsula met with a narrow path traced through the forest. Pursuing it, they came to an Indian village. "We stayed there a while and had of them strawberries and other thinges. . . . One of the Savages brought us on the way to the Woodside where there was a Garden of Tobacco and other fruits and herbes; he gathered Tobacco and distributed to every one of us, so wee departed."

It is evident that neither race yet knew if it

was to be war or peace. What the white man thought and came to think of the red man has been set down often enough; there is scantier testimony as to what was the red man's opinion of the white man. Here imagination must be called upon.

Newport's instructions from the London Council included exploration before he should leave the colonists and bring the three ships back to England. Now, with the pinnace and a score of men, among whom was John Smith, he went sixty miles up the river to where the flow is broken by a world of boulders and islets, to the hills crowned today by Richmond, capital of Virginia. The first adventurers called these rapid and whirling waters the Falls of the Farre West. To their notion they must lie at least half-way across the breadth of America. Misled by Indian stories, they believed and wrote that five or six days' march from the Falls of the Farre West, even through the thick forest, would bring them to the South Sea. The Falls of the Farre West, where at Richmond the James goes with a roaring sound around tree-crowned islets — it is strange to think that they once marked our frontier! How that frontier has been pushed westward is a romance indeed. And still, today, it is but a five or six days' journey to that South Sea sought by those early Virginians. The only condition for us is that we shall board a train. Tomorrow, with the airship, the South Sea may come nearer yet!

The Indians of this part of the earth were of the great Algonquin family, and the tribes with which the colonists had now to do were drawn, probably by a polity based on blood ties, into a loose confederation within the larger mass. Newport was told that the name of the river was Powhatan, the name of the chief Powhatan, and the name of the people Powhatans. But it seemed that the chief Powhatan was not at this village but at another and a larger place named Werowocomoco, on a second great river in the back country to the north and east of Jamestown. Newport and his men were "well entreated" by the Indians. "But yet," says Percy, "the Savages murmured at our planting in the Countrie."

The party did not tarry up the river. Back came their boat through the bright weather, between the verdurous banks, all green and flower-tinted save where might be seen the brown of Indian clearings with bark-covered huts and thin, up-curling blue smoke. Before them once more rose Jamestown, palisaded now, and riding before it the three ships. And here there barked an English dog, and here were Englishmen to welcome Englishmen. Both parties had news to tell, but the town had most. On the 26th of May, Indians had made an attack — four hundred of them with the Werowance of Paspihe. One Englishman had been killed, a number wounded. Four of the Council had each man his wound.

Newport must now lift anchor and sail away to England. He left at Jamestown a fort "having three Bulwarkes at every corner like a halfe Moone, and foure or five pieces of Artillerie mounted in them," a street or two of reed-thatched cabins, a church to match, a storehouse, a market-place and drill ground, and about all a stout palisade with a gate upon the river side. He left corn sown and springing high, and some food in the storehouse. And he left a hundred Englishmen who had now tasted of the country fare and might reasonably fear no worse chance than had yet befallen. Newport promised to return in twenty weeks with full supplies.

John Smith says that his enemies, chief amongst whom was Wingfield, would have sent him with Newport to England, there to stand trial for attempted mutiny, whereupon he demanded a trial in Virginia, and got it and was fully cleared. He now takes his place in the Council, beforetime denied him. He has good words only for Robert Hunt, the chaplain, who, he says, went from one to the other with the best of counsel. Were they not all here in the wilderness together, with the savages hovering about them like the Philistines about the Jews of old? How should the English live, unless among themselves they lived in amity? So for the moment factions were reconciled, and all went to church to partake of the Holy Communion.

Newport sailed, having in the holds of his ships sassafras and valuable woods but no gold to meet the London Council's hopes, nor any certain news of the South Sea. In due time he reached England, and in due time he turned and came again to Virginia. But long was the sailing to and fro between the daughter country and the mother country and the lading and unlading at either shore. It was seven months before Newport came again.

While he sails, and while England-in-America watches for him longingly, look for a moment at the attitude of Spain, falling old in the procession of world-powers, but yet with grip and cunning

left.   Spain misliked that English New World venture.   She wished to keep these seas for her own;
only, with waning energies, she could not always
enforce what she conceived to be her right.   By
now there was seen to be much clay indeed in the
image.   Philip the Second was dead; and Philip
the Third, an indolent king, lived in the Escurial.

Pedro de Zuñiga is the Spanish Ambassador to
the English Court.   He has orders from Philip to
keep him informed, and this he does, and from
time to time suggests remedies.   He writes of
Newport and the First Supply.   "Sire. . . .   Captain Newport makes haste to return with some
people — and there have combined merchants and
other persons who desire to establish themselves
there; because it appears to them the most suitable
place that they have discovered for privateering
and making attacks upon the merchant fleets of
Your Majesty.   Your Majesty will command to
see whether they will be allowed to remain there.
. . .   They are in a great state of excitement
about that place, and very much afraid lest Your
Majesty should drive them out of it. . . .   And
there are so many . . . who speak already of
sending people to that country, that it is advisable
not to be too slow; because they will soon be

found there with large numbers of people."[1]   In
Spain the Council of State takes action upon
Zuñiga's communications and closes a report to
the King with these words: "The actual taking
possession will be to drive out of Virginia all who
are there now, before they are reënforced, and
. . . it will be well to issue orders that the small
fleet stationed to the windward, which for so many
years has been in state of preparation, should be
instantly made ready and forthwith proceed to
drive out all who are now in Virginia, since their
small numbers will make this an easy task, and
this will suffice to prevent them from again coming
to that place." Upon this is made a Royal note:
"Let such measures be taken in this business as
may now and hereafter appear proper."

It would seem that there was cause indeed for
watching down the river by that small, small town
that was all of the United States! But there
follows a Spanish memorandum. "The driving
out . . . by the fleet stationed to the windward
will be postponed for a long time because delay
will be caused by getting it ready."[2]   Delay followed delay, and old Spain — *conquistador* Spain

---

[1] Brown's *Genesis of the United States,* vol. I, pp. 116–118.
[2] *Op. cit.,* vol. I, p. 127.

— grew older, and the speech on Jamestown Island is still English.

Christopher Newport was gone; no ships — the last refuges, the last possibilities for home-turning, should the earth grow too hard and the sky too black — rode upon the river before the fort. Here was the summer heat. A heavy breath rose from immemorial marshes, from the ancient floor of the forest. When clouds gathered and storms burst, they amazed the heart with their fearful thunderings and lightnings. The colonists had no well, but drank from the river, and at neither high nor low tide found the water whole-some. While the ships were here they had help of ship stores, but now they must subsist upon the grain that they had in the storehouse, now scant and poor enough. They might fish and hunt, but against such resources stood fever and inexperience and weakness, and in the woods the lurking sav-ages. The heat grew greater, the water worse, the food less. Sickness began. Work became toil. Men pined from homesickness, then, coming together, quarreled with a weak violence, then dropped away again into corners and sat listlessly with hanging heads.

The sixth of August there died John Asbie of the bloodie Flixe. The ninth day died George Flowre of the swelling. The tenth day died William Bruster gentleman, of a wound given by the Savages. . . . The fourteenth day Jerome Alikock, Ancient, died of a wound, the same day Francis Mid-winter, Edward Moris, Corporall, died suddenly. The fifteenth day their died Edward Browne and Stephen Galthrope. The sixteenth day their died Thomas Gower gentleman. The seventeenth day their died Thomas Mounslie. The eighteenth day theer died Robert Pennington and John Martine gentlemen. The nineteenth day died Drue Piggase gentleman.

The two and twentieth day of August there died Captain Bartholomew Gosnold one of our Councell, he was honourably buried having all the Ordnance in the Fort shot off, with many vollies of small shot. . . .

The foure and twentieth day died Edward Harrington and George Walker and were buried the same day. The six and twentieth day died Kenelme Throgmortine. The seven and twentieth day died William Roods. The eight and twentieth day died Thomas Stoodie, Cape Merchant. The fourth day of September died Thomas Jacob, Sergeant. The fifth day there died Benjamin Beast. . . ."[1]

Extreme misery makes men blind, unjust, and weak of judgment. Here was gross wretchedness, and the colonists proceeded to blame A and B and C, lost all together in the wilderness. It was this

[1] Percy's *Discourse*.

councilor or that councilor, this ambitious one or that one, this or that almost certainly ascertained traitor! Wanting to steal the pinnace, the one craft left by Newport, wanting to steal away in the pinnace and leave the mass — small enough mass now! — without boat or raft or straw to cling to, made the favorite accusation. Upon this count, early in September, Wingfield was deposed from the presidency. Ratcliffe succeeded him, but presently Ratcliffe fared no better. One councilor fared worse, for George Kendall, accused of plotting mutiny and pinnace stealing, was given trial, found guilty, and shot.

"The eighteenth day [of September] died one Ellis Kinistone. . . . The same day at night died one Richard Simmons. The nineteenth day there died one Thomas Mouton. . . ."

What went on, in Virginia, in the Indian mind, can only be conjectured. As little as the white mind could it foresee the trend of events or the ultimate outcome of present policy. There was exhibited a see-saw policy, or perhaps no policy at all, only the emotional fit as it came hot or cold. The friendly act trod upon the hostile, the hostile upon the friendly. Through the miserable summer the hostile was uppermost; then with the autumn appeared the friendly mood, fortunate enough for "the most feeble wretches" at Jamestown. Indians came laden with maize and venison. The heat was a thing of the past; cool and bracing weather appeared; and with it great flocks of wild fowl, "swans, geese, ducks and cranes." Famine vanished, sickness decreased. The dead were dead. Of the hundred and four persons left by Newport less than fifty had survived. But these may be thought of as indeed seasoned.

CHAPTER IV

JOHN SMITH

WITH the cool weather began active exploration, the object in chief the gathering from the Indians, by persuasion or trade or show of force, food for the approaching winter. Here John Smith steps forward as leader.

There begins a string of adventures of that hardy and romantic individual. How much in Smith's extant narrations is exaggeration, how much is dispossession of others' merits in favor of his own, it is difficult now to say.[1] A thing that one little likes is his persistent depreciation of his fellows. There is but one Noble Adventurer, and that one is John Smith. On the other hand evident enough are his courage and initiative, his

[1] Those who would strike John Smith from the list of historians will commend the author's caution to the reader before she lets the Captain tell his own tale. Whatever Smith may not have been, he was certainly a consummate *raconteur*. He belongs with the renowned story-tellers of the world, if not with the veracious chroniclers. — *Editor*.

ingenuity, and his rough, practical sagacity. Let us take him at something less than his own valuation, but yet as valuable enough. As for his adventures, real or fictitious, one may see in them epitomized the adventures of many and many men, English, French, Spanish, Dutch, blazers of the material path for the present civilization.

In December, rather autumn than winter in this region, he starts with the shallop and a handful of men up a tributary river that they have learned to call the Chickahominy. He is going for corn, but there is also an idea that he may hear news of that wished-for South Sea.

The Chickahominy proved itself a wonderland of swamp and tree-choked streams. Somewhere up its chequered reaches Smith left the shallop with men to guard it, and, taking two of the party with two Indian guides, went on in a canoe up a narrower way. Presently those left with the boat incautiously go ashore and are attacked by Indians. One is taken, tortured, and slain. The others get back to their boat and so away, down the Chickahominy and into the now somewhat familiar James. But Smith with his two men, Robinson and Emry, are now alone in the wilderness, up among narrow waters, brown marshes, fallen and obstructing tree trunks. Now come the men-hunting Indians — the King of Pamaunck, says Smith, with two hundred bowmen. Robinson and Emry are shot full of arrows. Smith is wounded, but with his musket deters the foe, killing several of the savages. His eyes upon them, he steps backward, hoping he may beat them off till he shall recover the shallop, but meets with the ill chance of a boggy and icy stream into which he stumbles, and here is taken.

See him now before "Opechancanough, King of Pamaunck!" Savages and procedures of the more civilized with savages have, the world over, a family resemblance. Like many a man before him and after, Smith casts about for a propitiatory wonder. He has with him, so fortunately, "a round ivory double-compass dial." This, with a genial manner, he would present to Opechancanough. The savages gaze, cannot touch through the glass the moving needle, grunt their admiration. Smith proceeds, with gestures and what Indian words he knows, to deliver a scientific lecture. Talking is best anyhow, will give them less time in which to think of those men he shot. He tells them that the world is round, and discourses about the sun and moon and stars and the alternation of day and night. He speaks with eloquence of the nations of the earth, of white men, yellow men, black men, and red men, of his own country and its grandeurs, and would explain antipodes.

Apparently all is waste breath and of no avail, for in an hour see him bound to a tree, a sturdy figure of a man, bearded and moustached, with a high forehead, clad in shirt and jerkin and breeches and hosen and shoon, all by this time, we may be sure, profoundly in need of repair. The tree and Smith are ringed by Indians, each of whom has an arrow fitted to his bow. Almost one can hear a knell ringing in the forest! But Opechancanough, moved by the compass, or willing to hear more of seventeenth-century science, raises his arm and stops the execution. Unbinding Smith, they take him with them as a trophy. Presently all reach their town of Orapaks.

Here he was kindly treated. He saw Indian dances, heard Indian orations. The women and children pressed about him and admired him greatly. Bread and venison were given him in such quantity that he feared that they meant to fatten and eat him. It is, moreover, dangerous to be considered powerful where one is scarcely so.

A young Indian lay mortally ill, and they took Smith to him and demanded that forthwith he be cured. If the white man could kill — how they were not able to see — he could likewise doubtless restore life. But the Indian presently died. His father, crying out in fury, fell upon the stranger who could have done so much and would not! Here also coolness saved the white man.

Smith was now led in triumph from town to town through the winter woods. The James was behind him, the Chickahominy also; he was upon new great rivers, the Pamunkey and the Rappahannock. All the villages were much alike, alike the still woods, the sere patches from which the corn had been taken, the bear, the deer, the foxes, the turkeys that were met with, the countless wild fowl. Everywhere were the same curious, crowding savages, the fires, the rustic cookery, the covering skins of deer and fox and otter, the oratory, the ceremonial dances, the manipulations of medicine men or priests — these last, to the Englishmen, pure "devils with antique tricks." Days were consumed in this going from place to place. At one point was produced a bag of gunpowder, gained in some way from Jamestown. It was being kept with care to go into the earth in the spring and produce, when summer came, some wonderful crop.

Opechancanough was a great chief, but higher than he moved Powhatan, chief of chiefs. This Indian was yet a stranger to the English in Virginia. Now John Smith was to make his acquaintance.

Werowocomoco stood upon a bluff on the north side of York River. Here came Smith and his captors, around them the winter woods, before them the broad blue river. Again the gathered Indians, men and women, again the staring, the handling, the more or less uncomplimentary remarks; then into the Indian ceremonial lodge he was pushed. Here sat the chief of chiefs, Powhatan, and he had on a robe of raccoon skins with all the tails hanging. About him sat his chief men, and behind these were gathered women. All were painted, head and shoulders; all wore, bound about the head, adornments meant to strike with beauty or with terror; all had chains of beads. Smith does not report what he said to Powhatan, or Powhatan to him. He says that the Queen of Appamatuck brought him water for his hands, and that there was made a great feast. When this was over, the Indians held a council. It

ended in a death decree. Incontinently Smith
was seized, dragged to a great stone lying before
Powhatan, forced down and bound. The Indians
made ready their clubs, meaning to batter his
brains out.   Then, says Smith, occurred the
miracle.

A child of Powhatan's, a very young girl called
Pocahontas, sprang from among the women, ran
to the stone, and with her own body sheltered that
of the Englishman. . . .[1]

What, in Powhatan's mind, of hesitation, wili-
ness, or good nature backed his daughter's plea is
not known. But Smith did not have his brains
beaten out. He was released, taken by some form
of adoption into the tribe, and set to using those
same brains in the making of hatchets and orna-
ments. A few days passed and he was yet further
enlarged. Powhatan longed for two of the great
guns possessed by the white men and for a grindstone. He would send Smith back to Jamestown
if in return he was sure of getting those treasures.
It is to be supposed that Smith promised him guns

[1] A vast amount of erudition has been expended by historical
students to establish the truth or falsity of this Pocahontas story.
The author has refrained from entering the controversy, preferring to
let the story stand as it was told by Captain Smith in his *General
History* (1624). — *Editor.*

and grindstones as many as could be borne away.

So Werowocomoco saw him depart, twelve Indians for escort. He had leagues to go, a night or two to spend upon the march. Lying in the huge winter woods, he expected, on the whole, death before morning. But "Almighty God mollified the hearts of those sterne barbarians with compassion." And so he was restored to Jamestown, where he found more dead than when he left. Some there undoubtedly welcomed him as a strong man restored when there was need of strong men. Others, it seems, would as lief that Pocahontas had not interfered.

The Indians did not get their guns and grindstones. But Smith loaded a demi-culverin with stones and fired upon a great tree, icicle-hung. The gun roared, the boughs broke, the ice fell rattling, the smoke spread, the Indians cried out and cowered away. Guns and grindstone, Smith told them, were too violent and heavy devils for them to carry from river to river. Instead he gave them, from the trading store, gifts enticing to the savage eye, and not susceptible of being turned against the donors.

Here at Jamestown in midwinter were more food and less mortal sickness than in the previous fearful summer, yet no great amount of food, and now suffering, too, from bitter cold. Nor had the sickness ended, nor dissensions. Less than fifty men were all that held together England and America — a frayed cord, the last strands of which might presently part. . . .

Then up the river comes Christopher Newport in the *Francis and John*, to be followed some weeks later by the *Phœnix*. Here is new life — stores for the settlers and a hundred new Virginians! How certain, at any rate, is the exchange of talk of home and hair-raising stories of this wilderness between the old colonists and the new! And certain is the relief and the renewed hopes. Mourning turns to joy. Even a conflagration that presently destroys the major part of the town can not blast that felicity.

Again Newport and Smith and others went out to explore the country. They went over to Werowocomoco and talked with Powhatan. He told them things which they construed to mean that the South Sea was near at hand, and they marked this down as good news for the home Council — still impatient for gold and Cathay. On their return to Jamestown they found under way new and stouter houses. The Indians were again friendly; they brought venison and turkeys and corn. Smith says that every few days came Pocahontas and attendant women bringing food.

Spring came again with the dogwood and the honeysuckle and the strawberries, the gay, returning birds, the barred and striped and mottled serpents. The colony was one year old. Back to England sailed the *Francis and John* and the *Phœnix*, carrying home Edward-Maria Wingfield, who has wearied of Virginia and will return no more.

What rests certain and praiseworthy in Smith is his thoroughness and daring in exploration. This summer he went with fourteen others down the river in an open boat, and so across the great bay, wide as a sea, to what is yet called the Eastern Shore, the counties now of Accomac and Northampton. Rounding Cape Charles these indefatigable explorers came upon islets beaten by the Atlantic surf. These they named Smith's Islands. Landing upon the main shore, they met "grimme and stout" savages, who took them to the King of Accomac, and him they found civil enough. This side of the great bay, with every creek and inlet, Smith examined and set down upon the map he was making. Even if he could find no gold for the Council at home, at least he would know what places were suited for "harbours and habitations." Soon a great storm came up, and they landed again, met yet other Indians, went farther, and were in straits for fresh water. The weather became worse; they were in danger of shipwreck — had to bail the boat continually. Indians gathered upon the shore and discharged flights of arrows, but were dispersed by a volley from the muskets. The bread the English had with them went bad. Wind and weather were adverse; three or four of the fifteen fell ill, but recovered. The weather improved; they came to the seven-mile-wide mouth of "Patawomeck" — the Potomac. They turned their boat up this vast stream. For a long time they saw upon the woody banks no savages. Then without warning they came upon ambuscades of great numbers "so strangely painted, grimed and disguised, shouting, yelling and crying, as we rather supposed them so many divils." Smith, in midstream, ordered musket-fire, and the balls went grazing over the water, and the terrible sound echoed through the woods. The savages threw down their bows and arrows and made signs of friendliness. The English went ashore, hostages were exchanged, and a kind of amicableness ensued. After such sylvan entertainment Smith and his men returned to the boat. The oars dipped and rose, the bright water broke from them; and these Englishmen in Old Virginia proceeded up the Potomac. Could they have seen — could they but have seen before them, on the north bank, rising, like the unsubstantial fabric of a dream, there above the trees, a vast, white Capitol shining in the sunlight!

Far up the river, they noticed that the sand on the shore gleamed with yellow spangles. They looked and saw high rocks, and they thought that from these the rain had washed the glittering dust. Gold? Harbors they had found — but what of gold? What, even, of Cathay?

Going down stream, they sought again those friendly Indians. Did they know gold or silver? The Indians looked wise, nodded heads, and took the visitors up a little tributary river to a rocky hill in which "with shells and hatchets" they had opened as it were a mine. Here they gathered a mineral which, when powdered, they sprinkled over themselves and their idols "making them," says the relation, "like blackamoors dusted over with silver." The white men filled their boat with as much of this ore as they could carry.

High were their hopes over it, but when it was subsequently sent to London and assayed, it was found to be worthless.

The fifteen now started homeward, out of Potomac and down the westward side of Chesapeake. In their travels they saw, besides the Indians, all manner of four-footed Virginians. Bears rolled their bulk through these forests; deer went whither they would. The explorers might meet foxes and catamounts, otter, beaver and marten, raccoon and opossum, wolf and Indian dog. Winged Virginians made the forests vocal. The owl hooted at night, and the whippoorwill called in the twilight. The streams were filled with fish. Coming to the mouth of the Rappahannock, the travelers' boat grounded upon sand, with the tide at ebb. Awaiting the water that should lift them off, the fifteen began with their swords to spear the fish among the reeds. Smith had the ill luck to encounter a sting-ray, and received its barbed weapon through his wrist. There set in a great swelling and torment which made him fear that death was at hand. He ordered his funeral and a grave to be dug on a neighboring islet. Yet by degrees he grew better and so out of torment, and withal so hungry that he longed for supper, whereupon, with a light heart, he had his late enemy the sting-ray cooked and ate him. They then named the place Sting-ray Island and, the tide serving, got off the sand-bar and down the bay, and so came home to Jamestown, having been gone seven weeks.

Like Ulysses, Smith refuses to rust in inaction. A few days, and away he is again, first up to Rappahannock, and then across the bay. On this journey he and his men come up with the giant Susquehannocks, who are not Algonquins but Iroquois. After many hazards in which the forest and the savage play their part, Smith and his band again return to Jamestown. In all this adventuring they have gained much knowledge of the country and its inhabitants — but yet no gold, and no further news of the South Sea or of far Cathay.

It was now September and the second summer with its toll of fever victims was well-nigh over. Autumn and renewed energy were at hand. All the land turned crimson and gold. At Jamestown building went forward, together with the gathering of ripened crops, the felling of trees, fishing and fowling, and trading for Indian corn and turkeys.

One day George Percy, heading a trading party down the river, saw coming toward him a white-

sailed ship, the *Mary and Margaret* — it was Christopher Newport again, with the second supply.
Seventy colonists came over on the *Mary and
Margaret*, among them a fair number of men of
note.   Here were Captain Peter Wynne and Richard Waldo, "old soldiers and valiant gentlemen,"
Francis West, young brother of the Lord De La
Warr, Rawley Crashaw, John Codrington, Daniel
Tucker, and others.   This is indeed an important
ship.   Among the laborers, the London Council
had sent eight Poles and Germans, skilled in their
own country in the production of pitch, tar, glass,
and soap-ashes.   Here, then, begin in Virginia
other blood strains than the English.   And in the
Mary and Margaret comes with Master Thomas
Forest his wife, Mistress Forest, and her maid,
by name Anne Burras.   Apart from those lost ones
of Raleigh's colony at Roanoke, these are the first
Englishwomen in Virginia.   There may be guessed
what welcome they got, how much was made of
them.

Christopher Newport had from that impatient
London Council somewhat strange orders.   He
was not to return without a lump of gold, or a
certain discovery of waters pouring into the South
Sea, or some notion gained of the fate of the lost

colony of Roanoke. He had been given a barge which could be taken to pieces and so borne around those Falls of the Far West, then put together, and the voyage to the Pacific resumed. Moreover, he had for Powhatan, whom the minds at home figured as a sort of Asiatic Despot, a gilt crown and a fine ewer and basin, a bedstead, and a gorgeous robe.

The easiest task, that of delivering Powhatan's present and placing an idle crown upon that Indian's head who, among his own people, was already sufficiently supreme, might be and was performed. And Newport with a large party went again to the Falls of the Far West and miles deep into the country beyond. Here they found Indians outside the Powhatan Confederacy, but no South Sea, nor mines of gold and silver, nor any news of the lost colony of Roanoke. In December Newport left Virginia in the *Mary and Margaret*, and with him sailed Ratcliffe. Smith succeeded to the presidency.

About this time John Laydon, a laborer, and Anne Burras, that maid of Mistress Forest's, fell in love and would marry. So came about the first English wedding in Virginia.

Winter followed with snow and ice, nigh two

hundred people to feed, and not overmuch in the larder with which to do it. Smith with George Percy and Francis West and others went again to the Indians for corn. Christmas found them weather-bound at Kecoughtan. "Wherever an Englishman may be, and in whatever part of the world, he must keep Christmas with feasting and merriment! And, indeed, we were never more merrie, nor fedde on more plentie of good oysters, fish, flesh, wild fowle and good bread; nor never had better fires in England than in the drie, smokie houses of Kecoughtan!"

But despite this Christmas fare, there soon began quarrels, many and intricate, with Powhatan and his brother Opechancanough.

CHAPTER V

THE "SEA ADVENTURE"

EXPERIENCE is a great teacher. That London Company with Virginia to colonize had now come to see how inadequate to the attempt were its means and strength. Evidently it might be long before either gold mines or the South Sea could be found. The company's ships were too slight and few; colonists were going by the single handful when they should go by the double. Something was at fault in the management of the enterprise. The quarrels in Virginia were too constant, the disasters too frequent. More money, more persons interested with purse and mind, a great company instead of a small, a national cast to the enterprise — these were imperative needs. In the press of such demands the London Company passed away. In 1609 under new letters patent was born the Virginia Company.

The members and shareholders in this corporation touch through and through the body of England at that day. First names upon the roll come Robert Cecil, Thomas Howard, Henry Wriothesley, William Herbert, Henry Clinton, Richard Sackville, Thomas Cecil, Philip Herbert — Earls of Salisbury, Suffolk, Southampton, Pembroke, Lincoln, Dorset, Exeter, and Montgomery. Then follow a dozen peers, the Lord Bishop of Bath and Wells, a hundred knights, many gentlemen, one hundred and ten merchants, certain physicians and clergymen, old soldiers of the Continental wars, sea-captains and mariners, and a small host of the unclassified. In addition shares were taken by fifty-six London guilds or industrial companies. Here are the Companies of the Tallow and Wax Chandlers, the Armorers and Girdlers, Cordwayners and Carpenters, Masons, Plumbers, Founders, Poulterers, Cooks, Coopers, Tylers and Brick Layers, Bowyers and Vinters, Merchant Taylors, Blacksmiths and Weavers, Mercers, Grocers, Turners, Gardeners, Dyers, Scriveners, Fruiterers, Plaisterers, Brown Bakers, Imbroiderers, Musicians, and many more.

The first Council appointed by the new charter had fifty-two members, fourteen of whom sat in the English House of Lords, and twice that number in the Commons. Thus was Virginia well linked to Crown and Parliament.

This great commercial company had sovereign powers within Virginia. The King should have his fifth part of all ore of gold and silver; the laws and religion of England should be upheld, and no man let go to Virginia who had not first taken the oath of supremacy. But in the wide field beside all this the President — called the Treasurer — and the Council, henceforth to be chosen out of and by the whole body of subscribers, had full sway. No longer should there be a second Council sitting in Virginia, but a Governor with power, answerable only to the Company at home. That Company might tax and legislate within the Virginian field, punish the ill-doer or "rebel," and wage war, if need be, against Indian or Spaniard.

One of the first actions of the newly constituted body was to seek remedy for the customary passage by way of the West Indies — so long and so beset by dangers. They sent forth a small ship under Captain Samuel Argall, with instructions "to attempt a direct and cleare passage, by leaving the Canaries to the East, and from thence to run a straight westerne course. . . . And so to make an experience of the Winds and

Currents which have affrighted all undertakers by the North."

This Argall, a young man with a stirring and adventurous life behind him and before him, took his ship the indicated way. He made the voyage in nine weeks, of which two were spent becalmed, and upon his return reported that it might be made in seven, "and no apparent inconvenience in the way." He brought to the great Council of the Company a story of necessity and distress at Jamestown, and the Council lays much of the blame for that upon "the misgovernment of the Commanders, by dissention and ambition among themselves," and upon the idleness of the general run, "active in nothing but adhearing to factions and parts." The Council, sitting afar from a savage land, is probably much too severe. But the "factions and parts" cannot easily be denied.

Before Argall's return, the Company had commissioned as Governor of Virginia Sir Thomas Gates, and had gathered a fleet of seven ships and two pinnaces with Sir George Somers as Admiral, in the ship called the *Sea Adventure*, and Christopher Newport as Vice-Admiral. All weighed anchor from Falmouth early in June and sailed by the newly tried course, south to the Canaries and then across. These seven ships carried five hundred colonists, men, women, and children.

On St. James's day there rose and broke a fearsome storm. Two days and nights it raged, and it scattered that fleet of seven. Gates, Somers, and Newport with others of "rancke and quality" were upon the *Sea Adventure.* How fared this ship with one attendant pinnace we shall come to see presently. But the other ships, driven to and fro, at last found a favorable wind, and in August they sighted Virginia. On the eleventh of that month they came, storm-beaten and without Governor or Admiral or *Sea Adventure,* into "our Bay" and at last to "the King's River and Town." Here there swarmed from these ships nigh three hundred persons, meeting and met by the hundred dwelling at Jamestown. This was the third supply, but it lacked the hundred or so upon the *Sea Adventure* and the pinnace, and it lacked a head. "Being put ashore without their Governor or any order from him (all the Commissioners and principal persons being aboard him) no man would acknowledge a superior."

With this multitude appeared once more in Virginia the three ancient councilors — Ratcliffe, Archer, and Martin. Apparently here came fresh fuel for factions. Who should rule, and who should be ruled? Here is an extremely old and important question, settled in history only to be unsettled again. Everywhere it rises, dust on Time's road, and is laid only to rise again.

Smith was still President. Who was in the right and who in the wrong in these ancient quarrels, the recital of which fills the pages of Smith and of other men, is hard now to be determined. But Jamestown became a place of turbulence. Francis West was sent with a considerable number to the Falls of the Far West to make there some kind of settlement. For a like purpose Martin and Percy were dispatched to the Nansemond River. All along the line there was bitter falling out. The Indians became markedly hostile. Smith was up the river, quarreling with West and his men. At last he called them "wrongheaded asses," flung himself into his boat, and made down the river to Jamestown. Yet even so he found no peace, for, while he was asleep in the boat, by some accident or other a spark found its way to his powder pouch. The powder exploded. Terribly hurt, he leaped overboard into the river, whence he was with difficulty rescued.

Smith was now deposed by Ratcliffe, Archer, and

Martin, because, "being an ambityous, onworthy, and vayneglorious fellowe," say his detractors, "he wolde rule all and ingrose all authority into his own hands." Be this as it may, Smith was put on board one of the ships which were about to sail for England. Wounded, and with none at Jamestown able to heal his hurt, he was no unwilling passenger. Thus he departed, and Virginia knew Captain John Smith no more. Some liked him and his ways, some liked him not nor his ways either. He wrote of his own deeds and praised them highly, and saw little good in other mankind, though here and there he made an exception. Evident enough are faults of temper. But he had great courage and energy and at times a lofty disinterestedness.

Again winter drew on at Jamestown, and with it misery on misery. George Percy, now President, lay ill and unable to keep order. The multitude, "unbridled and heedless," pulled this way and that. Before the cold had well begun, what provision there was in the storehouse became exhausted. That stream of corn from the Indians in which the colonists had put dependence failed to flow. The Indians themselves began systematically to spoil and murder. Ratcliffe and fourteen with him met death while loading his barge with corn upon the Pamunkey. The cold grew worse. By midwinter there was famine. The four hundred — already noticeably dwindled — dwindled fast and faster. The cold was severe; the Indians were in the woods; the weakened bodies of the white men pined and shivered. They broke up the empty houses to make fires to warm themselves. They began to die of hunger as well as by Indian arrows. On went the winter, and every day some died. Tales of cannibalism are told. . . . This was the Starving Time.

When the leaves were red and gold, England-in-America had a population of four hundred and more. When the dogwood and the strawberry bloomed, England-in-America had a population of but sixty.

Somewhat later than this time there came from the pen of Shakespeare a play dealing with a tempest and shipwreck and a magical isle and rescue thereon. The bright spirit Ariel speaks of "the still-vex'd Bermoothes." These were islands "two hundred leagues from any continent," named after a Spanish Captain Bermudez who had landed there. Once there had been Indians, but these the Spaniards had slain or taken as slaves. Now the islands were desolate, uninhabited, "forlorn and unfortunate." Chance vessels might touch, but the approach was dangerous. There grew rumors of pirates, and then of demons. "The Isles of Demons," was the name given to them. "The most forlorn and unfortunate place in the world" was the description that fitted them in those distant days:

> All torment, trouble, wonder and amazement
> Inhabits here: some heavenly power guide us
> Out of this fearful country.

When Shakespeare so wrote, there was news in England and talk went to and fro of the shipwreck of the *Sea Adventure* upon the rocky teeth of the Bermoothes, "uninhabitable and almost inaccessible," and of the escape and dwelling there for months of Gates and Somers and the colonists in that ship. It is generally assumed that this incident furnished timber for the framework of *The Tempest.*

The storm that broke on St. James's Day, scattering the ships of the third supply, drove the *Sea Adventure* here and there at will. Upon her watched Gates and Somers and Newport, above a hundred men, and a few women and children. There sprang a leak; all thought of death. Then rose a cry "Land ho!" The storm abated, but the wind carried the *Sea Adventure* upon this shore and grounded her upon a reef. A certain R. Rich, gentleman, one of the voyagers, made and published a ballad upon the whole event. If it is hardly Shakespearean music, yet it is not devoid of interest.

> . . . The Seas did rage, the windes did blowe,
>   Distressed were they then;
> Their shippe did leake, her tacklings breake,
>   In daunger were her men;
> But heaven was pylotte in this storme,
>   And to an Iland neare,
> Bermoothawes called, conducted them,
>   Which did abate their feare.

Using the ship's boats they got to shore, though with toil and danger. Here they found no sprites nor demons, nor even men, but a fair, half-tropical verdure and, running wild, great numbers of swine.

> And then on shoare the iland came
>   Inhabited by hogges,
> Some Foule and tortoyses there were,
>   They only had one dogge,

> To kill these swyne, to yield them foode,
>   That little had to eate.
> Their store was spent and all things scant,
>   Alas! they wanted meate.

They did not, however, starve.

> A thousand hogges that dogge did kill
>   Their hunger to sustaine.

Ten months the Virginia colonists lived among the "still-vex'd Bermoothes." The *Sea Adventure* was but a wreck pinned between the reefs. No sail was seen upon the blue water. Where they were thrown, there Gates and Somers and Newport and all must stay for a time and make the best of it. They builded huts and thatched them, and they brought from the wrecked ship, pinned but half a mile from land, stores of many kinds. The clime proved of the blandest, fairest; with fishing and hunting they maintained themselves. Days, weeks, and months went by. They had a minister, Master Buck. They brought from the ship a bell and raised it for a church-bell. A marriage, a few deaths, the birth of two children — these were events on the island. One of these children, the daughter of John Rolfe, gentleman, and his wife, was christened Bermuda. Gates and

Somers held kindly sway. The colonists lived in plenty, peace, and ease. But for all that, they were shipwrecked folk, and far, far out of the world, and they longed for the old ways and their own kin. Day followed day, but no sail would show to bear them thence; and so at last, taking what they could from the forests of the island, and from the *Sea Adventure*, they set about to become shipwrights.

> And there two gallant pynases,
>   Did build of Seader-tree,
> The brave *Deliverance* one was call'd,
>   Of seaventy tonne was shee,
> The other *Patience* had to name,
>   Her burthen thirty tonne. . . .
>
> . . . The two and forty weekes being past
>   They hoyst sayle and away;
> Their shippes with hogges well freighted were,
>   Their harts with mickle joy.
>
> And so to Virginia came . . .

What they found when they came to Virginia was dolor enough. On Jamestown strand they beheld sixty skeletons "who had eaten all the quick things that weare there, and some of them had eaten snakes and adders." Somers, Gates, and Newport, on entering the town, found it "rather as the ruins of some auntient fortification than that any people living might now inhabit it."

A pitiable outcome, this, of all the hopes of fair "harbours and habitations," of golden dreams, and far-flung dominion. All those whom Raleigh had sent to Roanoke were lost or had perished. Those who had named and had first dwelled in Jamestown were in number about a hundred. To these had been added, during the first year or so, perhaps two hundred more. And the ships that had parted from the *Sea Adventure* had brought in three hundred. First and last, not far from seven hundred English folk had come to live in Virginia. And these skeletons eating snakes and adders were all that remained of that company; all those others had died miserably and their hopes were ashes with them.

What might Sir Thomas Gates, the Governor, do? "That which added most to his sorowe, and not a little startled him, was the impossibilitie . . . how to amend one whitt of this. His forces were not of habilitie to revenge upon the Indian, nor his owne supply (now brought from the Bermudas) sufficient to relieve his people." So he called a Council and listened in turn to Sir George Somers, to Christopher Newport, and to "the gentlemen and Counsaile of the former Government." The end and upshot was that none could see other course than to abandon the country. England-in-America had tried and failed, and had tried again and failed. God, or the course of Nature, or the current of History was against her. Perhaps in time stronger forces and other attempts might yet issue from England. But now the hour had come to say farewell!

Upon the bosom of the river swung two pinnaces, the *Discovery* and the *Virginia*, left by the departing ships months before, and the *Deliverance* and the *Patience*, the Bermuda pinnaces. Thus the English abandoned the little town that was but three years old. Aboard the four small ships they went, and down the broad river, between the flowery shores, they sailed away. Doubtless under the trees on either hand were Indians watching this retreat of the invaders of their forests. The plan of the departing colonists was to turn north, when they had reached the sea, and make for Newfoundland, where they might perhaps meet with English fishing ships. So they sailed down the river, and doubtless many hearts were heavy and sad, but others doubtless were full of joy and thankfulness to be going back to an older home than Virginia.

The river broadened toward Chesapeake — and then, before them, what did they see? What deliverance for those who had held on to the uttermost? They saw the long boat of an English ship coming toward them with flashing oars, bringing news of comfort and relief. There, indeed, off Point Comfort lay three ships, the *De La Warr*, the *Blessing*, and the *Hercules*, and they brought, with a good company and good stores, Sir Thomas West, Lord De La Warr, appointed, over Gates, Lord Governor and Captain-General, by land and sea, of the Colony of Virginia.

The *Discovery*, the *Virginia*, the *Patience*, and the *Deliverance* thereupon put back to that shore they thought to have left forever. Two days later, on Sunday the 10th of June, 1610, there anchored before Jamestown the *De La Warr*, the *Blessing*, and the *Hercules;* and it was thus that the new Lord Governor wrote home: "I . . . in the afternoon went ashore, where after a sermon made by Mr. Buck . . . I caused my commission to be read, upon which Sir Thomas Gates delivered up unto me his owne commission, both patents, and the counsell seale; and then I delivered some few wordes unto the Company . . . and after . . . did constitute and give place of office and chardge to divers Captaines and gentlemen and elected unto me a counsaile."

The dead was alive again.   Saith Rich's ballad:

> And to the adventurers[1] thus he writes,
>   "Be not dismayed at all,
> For scandall cannot doe us wrong,
>   God will not let us fall.
> Let England knowe our willingnesse,
>   For that our worke is good,
> *We hope to plant a nation*
>   *Where none before hath stood.*"

[1] The Virginia Company.

CHAPTER VI

SIR THOMAS DALE

In a rebuilded Jamestown, Lord De La Warr, of "approved courage, temper and experience," held for a short interval dignified, seigneurial sway, while his restless associates adventured far and wide. Sir George Somers sailed back to the Bermudas to gather a cargo of the wild swine of those woods, but illness seized him there, and he died among the beautiful islands. That Captain Samuel Argall who had traversed for the Company the short road from the Canaries took up Smith's fallen mantle and carried on the work of exploration. It was he who found, and named for the Lord Governor, Delaware Bay. He went up the Potomac and traded for corn; rescued an English boy from the Indians; had brushes with the savages. In the autumn back to England with a string of ships went that tried and tested seafarer Christopher Newport. Virginia wanted many things, and chiefly that the Virginia Company should excuse defect and remember promise. So Gates sailed with Newport to make true report and guide exertion. Six months passed, and the Lord Governor himself fell ill and must home to England. So away he, too, went and for seven years until his death ruled from that distance through a deputy governor. De La Warr was a man of note and worth, old privy councilor of Elizabeth and of James, soldier in the Low Countries, strong Protestant and believer in England-in-America. Today his name is borne by a great river, a great bay, and by one of the United States.

In London, the Virginia Company, having listened to Gates, projected a fourth supply for the colony. Of those hundreds who had perished in Virginia, many had been true and intelligent men, and again many perhaps had been hardly that. But the Virginia Company was now determined to exercise for the future a discrimination. It issued a broadside, making known that it was sending a new supply of men and all necessary provision in a fleet of good ships, under the conduct of Sir Thomas Gates and Sir Thomas Dale, and that it was not intended any more to burden the action with "vagrant and unnecessary persons

. . . but honest and industrious men, as Carpenters, Smiths, Coopers, Fishermen, Tanners, Shoemakers, Shipwrights, Brickmen, Gardeners, Husbandmen, and laboring men of all sorts that . . . shall be entertained for the Voyage upon such termes as their qualitie and fitnesse shall deserve." Yet, in spite of precautions, some of the other sort continued to creep in with the sober and industrious. Master William Crashaw, in a sermon upon the Virginia venture, remarks that "they who goe . . . be like (for aught I see) to those who are left behind, even of all sorts better and worse!" This probably hits the mark.

The Virginia Company meant at last to have order in Virginia. To this effect, a new office was created and a strong man was found to fill it. Gates remained De La Warr's deputy governor, but Sir Thomas Dale went as Marshal of Virginia. The latter sailed in March, 1611, with "three ships, three hundred people, twelve kine, twenty goats, and all things needful for the colony." Gates followed in May with other ships, three hundred colonists, and much cattle.

For the next few years Dale becomes, in effect, ruler of Virginia. He did much for the colony, and therefore, in that far past that is not so dis-

tant either, much for the United States — a man
of note, and worth considering.

Dale had seen many years of service in the Low
Countries. He was still in Holland when the sum-
mons came to cross the ocean in the service of the
Virginia Company. On the recommendation of
Henry, Prince of Wales, the States-General of the
United Netherlands consented "that Captain
Thomas Dale (destined by the King of Great
Britain to be employed in Virginia in his Majesty's
service) may absent himself from his company for
the space of three years, and that his said company
shall remain meanwhile vacant, to be resumed by
him if he think proper."

This man had a soldier's way with him and an
iron will. For five years in Virginia he exhibited
a certain stern efficiency which was perhaps the
best support and medicine that could have been
devised. At the end of that time, leaving Virginia,
he did not return to the Dutch service, but became
Admiral of the fleet of the English East India
Company, thus passing from one huge historic
mercantile company to another. With six ships
he sailed for India. Near Java, the English and
the Dutch having chosen to quarrel, he had with
a Dutch fleet "a cruel, bloody fight." Later,

when peace was restored, the East India Company would have given him command of an allied fleet of English and Dutch ships, the objective being trade along the coast of Malabar and an attempt to open commerce with the Chinese. But Sir Thomas Dale was opening commerce with a vaster, hidden land, for at Masulipatam he died. "*Whose valor,*" says his epitaph, "*having shined in the Westerne, was set in the Easterne India.*"

But now in Maytime of 1611 Dale was in Virginian waters. By this day, beside the main settlement of Jamestown, there were at Cape Henry and Point Comfort small forts garrisoned with meager companies of men. Dale made pause at these, setting matters in order, and then, proceeding up the river, he came to Jamestown and found the people gathered to receive him. Presently he writes home to the Company a letter that gives a view of the place and its needs. Any number of things must be done, requiring continuous and hard work, "as, namely, the reparation of the falling Church and so of the Store-house, a stable for our horses, a munition house, a Powder house, a new well for the amending of the most unwholesome water which the old afforded. Brick to be made, a sturgion house . . . a Block house to be

raised on the North side of our back river to
prevent the Indians from killing our cattle, a
house to be set up to lodge our cattle in the winter,
and hay to be appointed in his due time to be
made, a smith's forge to be perfected — caske for
our Sturgions to be made, and besides private
gardens for each man common gardens for hemp
and flax and such other seeds, and lastly a bridge
to land our goods dry and safe upon, for most of
which I take present order."

Dale would have agreed with **Dr. Watts** that

> Satan finds some mischief still
> For idle hands to do!

If we of the United States today will call to
mind certain Western small towns of some decades
ago — if we will review them as they are pictured
in poem and novel and play — we may receive, as
it were out of the tail of the eye, an impression of
some aspects of these western plantings of the seventeenth century. The dare-devil, the bully, the
tenderfoot, the gambler, the gentleman-desperado
had their counterparts in Virginia. So had the cool,
indomitable sheriff and his dependable posse, the
friends generally of law and order. Dale may be
viewed as the picturesque sheriff of this earlier age.

But it must be remembered that this Virginia was of the seventeenth, not of the nineteenth century. And law had cruel and idiot faces as well as faces just and wise. Hitherto the colony possessed no written statutes. The Company now resolved to impose upon the wayward an iron restraint. It fell to Dale to enforce the regulations known as "Lawes and Orders, dyvine, politique, and martiall for the Colonye of Virginia" — not English civil law simply, but laws "chiefly extracted out of the Lawes for governing the army in the Low Countreys." The first part of this code was compiled by William Strachey; the latter part is thought to have been the work of Sir Edward Cecil, Sir Thomas Gates, and Dale himself, approved and accepted by the Virginia Company. Ten years afterwards, defending itself before a Committee of Parliament, the Company through its Treasurer declared "the necessity of such laws, in some cases *ad terrorem*, and in some to be truly executed."

Seventeenth-century English law herself was terrible enough in all conscience, but "Dale's Laws" went beyond. Offences ranged from failure to attend church and idleness to *lèse majesté*. The penalties were gross — cruel whippings, imprison-

ments, barbarous puttings to death. The High
Marshal held the unruly down with a high hand.

But other factors than this Draconian code
worked at last toward order in this English West.
Dale was no small statesman, and he played ferment against ferment. Into Virginia now first
came private ownership of land.[1] So much was
given to each colonist, and care of this booty became to each a preoccupation. The Company at
home sent out more and more settlers, and more
and more of the industrious, peace-loving sort.
By 1612 the English in America numbered about
eight hundred. Dale projected another town, and
chose for its site the great horseshoe bend in the
river a few miles below the Falls of the Far West,
at a spot we now call Dutch Gap. Here Dale laid
out a town which he named Henricus after the
Prince of Wales, and for its citizens he drafted
from Jamestown three hundred persons. To him
also are due Bermuda and Shirley Hundreds and
Dale's Gift over on the Eastern Shore. As the
Company sent over more colonists, there began to

---

[1] Hitherto there had been no trading or landholding by individuals.
All the colonists contributed the products of their toil to the common
store and received their supplies from the Company. The adventurers
(stockholders) contributed money to the enterprise; the colonists,
themselves and their labor.

show, up and down the James though at far intervals, cabins and clearings made by white men, set about with a stockade, and at the river edge a rude landing and a fastened boat. The restless search for mines of gold and silver now slackened. Instead eyes turned for wealth to the kingdom of the plant and tree, and to fur trade and fisheries.

Those ships that brought colonists were in every instance expected to return to England laden with the commodities of Virginia. At first cargoes of precious ores were looked for. These failing, the Company must take from Virginia what lay at hand and what might be suited to English needs. In 1610 the Company issued a paper of instructions upon this subject of Virginia commodities. The daughter was expected to send to the mother country sassafras root, bay berries, puccoon, sarsaparilla, walnut, chestnut, and chinquapin oil, wine, silk grass, beaver cod, beaver and otter skins, clapboard of oak and walnut, tar, pitch, turpentine, and powdered sturgeon.

It might seem that Virginia was headed to become a land of fishers, of foresters, and vine dressers, perhaps even, when the gold should be at last discovered, of miners. At home, the colonizing merchants and statesmen looked for some such

thing. In return for what she laded into ships,
Virginia was to receive English-made goods, and
to an especial degree woolen goods, "a very liber-
all utterance of our English cloths into a maine
country described to be bigger than all Europe."
There was to be direct trade, country kind for
country kind, and no specie to be taken out of
England. The promoters at home doubtless conceived a hardy and simple trans-Atlantic folk of
their own kindred, planters for their own needs,
steady consumers of the plainer sort of English
wares, steady gatherers, in return, of necessaries
for which England otherwise must trade after a
costly fashion with lands which were not always
friendly. A simple, sturdy, laborious Virginia,
white men and Indians — if this was their dream,
reality was soon to modify it.

A new commodity of unsuspected commercial
value began now to be grown in garden-plots along
the James — the "weed" *par excellence*, tobacco.
That John Rolfe who had been shipwrecked on
the *Sea Adventure* was now a planter in Virginia.
His child Bermuda had died in infancy, and his
wife soon after their coming to Jamestown. Rolfe
remained, a young man, a good citizen, and a Chris-

tian. And he loved tobacco. On that trivial fact hinges an important chapter in the economic history of America. In 1612 Rolfe planted tobacco in his own garden, experimented with its culture, and prophesied that the Virginian weed would rank with the best Spanish. It was now a shorter plant, smaller-leafed and smaller-flowered, but time and skilful gardening would improve it.

England had known tobacco for thirty years, owing its introduction to Raleigh. At first merely amused by the New World rarity, England was now by general use turning a luxury into a necessity. More and more she received through Dutch and Spanish ships tobacco from the Indies. Among the English adventurers to Virginia some already knew the uses of the weed; others soon learned from the Indians. Tobacco was perhaps not indigenous to Virginia, but had probably come through southern tribes who in turn had gained it from those who knew it in its tropic habitat. Now, however, tobacco was grown by all Virginia Indians, and was regarded as the Great Spirit's best gift. In the final happy hunting-ground, kings, werowances, and priests enjoyed it forever. When, in the time after the first landing, the Indians brought gifts to the adventurers as to beings from a superior sphere, they offered tobacco as well as comestibles like deer-meat and mulberries. Later, in England and in Virginia, there was some suggestion that it might be cultivated among other commodities. But the Company, not to be diverted from the path to profits, demanded from Virginia necessities and not new-fangled luxuries. Nevertheless, a little tobacco was sent over to England, and then a little more, and then a larger quantity. In less than five years it had become a main export; and from that time to this profoundly has it affected the life of Virginia and, indeed, of the United States.

This then is the wide and general event with which John Rolfe is connected. But there is also a narrower, personal happening that has pleased all these centuries. Indian difficulties yet abounded, but Dale, administrator as well as man of Mars, wound his way skilfully through them all. Powhatan brooded to one side, over there at Werowocomoco. Captain Samuel Argall was again in Virginia, having brought over sixty-two colonists in his ship, the *Treasurer*. A bold and restless man, explorer no less than mariner, he again went trading up the Potomac, and visited upon its banks the village of Japazaws, kinsman of Powhatan. Here he found no less a personage than Powhatan's daughter Pocahontas. An idea came into Argall's active and somewhat unscrupulous brain. He bribed Japazaws with a mighty gleaming copper kettle, and by that chief's connivance took Pocahontas from the village above the Potomac. He brought her captive in his boat down the Chesapeake to the mouth of the James and so up the river to Jamestown, here to be held hostage for an Indian peace. This was in 1613.

Pocahontas stayed by the James, in the rude settlers' town, which may have seemed to the Indian girl stately and wonderful enough. Here Rolfe made her acquaintance, here they talked together, and here, after some scruples on his part as to "heathennesse," they were married. He writes of "her desire to be taught and instructed in the knowledge of God; her capableness of understanding; her aptnesse and willingnesse to recieve anie good impression, and also the spiritual, besides her owne incitements stirring me up hereunto." First she was baptized, receiving the name Rebecca, and then she was married to Rolfe in the flower-decked church at Jamestown. Powhatan was not there, but he sent young chiefs, her brothers, in his place.

Rolfe had lands and cabins thereupon up the river near Henricus. He called this place Varina, the best Spanish tobacco being Varinas. Here he and Pocahontas dwelled together "civilly and lovingly." When two years had passed the couple went with their infant son upon a visit to England. There court and town and country flocked to see the Indian "princess." After a time she and Rolfe would go back to Virginia. But at Gravesend, before their ship sailed, she was stricken with smallpox and died, making "a religious and godly end," and there at Gravesend she is buried. Her son, Thomas Rolfe, who was brought up in England, returned at last to Virginia and lived out his life there with his wife and children. Today no small host of Americans have for ancestress the daughter of Powhatan. In England-in-America the immediate effect of the marriage was really to procure an Indian peace outlasting Pocahontas's brief life.

In Dale's years there rises above the English horizon the cloud of New France. The old, disaster-haunted Huguenot colony in Florida was a thing of the past, to be mourned for when the Spaniard wiped it out — for at that time England herself was not in America. But now that she was established there, with some hundreds of men in a Virginia that stretched from Spanish Florida to Nova Scotia, the French shadow seemed ominous. And just in this farther region, amid fir-trees and snow, upon the desolate Bay of Fundy, the French for some years had been keeping the breath of life in a huddle of cabins named Port Royal. More than this, and later than the Port Royal building, Frenchmen — Jesuits at that! — were trying a settlement on an island now called Mount Desert, off a coast now named Maine. The Virginia Company — doubtless with some reference back to the King and Privy Council — De La Warr, Gates, the deputy governor, and Dale, the High Marshal, appear to have been of one mind as to these French settlements. Up north there was still Virginia — in effect, England! Hands off, therefore, all European peoples speaking with an un-English tongue!

Now it happened about this time that Captain Samuel Argall received a commission "to go fishing," and that he fished off that coast that is now the coast of Maine, and brought his ship to anchor by Mount Desert. Argall, a swift and high-handed person, fished on dry land. He swept into his net the Jesuits on Mount Desert, set half of them in an open boat to meet with what ship they might, and brought the other half captive to Jamestown. Later, he appeared before Port Royal, where he burned the cabins, slew the cattle, and drove into the forest the settler Frenchmen. But Port Royal and the land about it called Acadia, though much hurt, survived Argall's fishing.[1]

There was also on Virginia in these days the shadow of Spain. In 1611 the English had found upon the beach near Point Comfort three Spaniards from a Spanish caravel which, as the Englishmen had learned with alarm, "was fitted with a shallop necessarie and propper to discover freshetts, rivers, and creekes." They took the three prisoner and applied for instructions to Dale, who held them to be spies and clapped them into prison at Point Comfort.

That Dale's suspicions were correct, is proved by a letter which the King of Spain wrote in cipher to the Spanish Ambassador in London ordering him to confer with the King as to the liberty of three prisoners whom Englishmen in Virginia have captured. The three are "the Alcayde Don Diego de Molino, Ensign Marco Antonio Perez,

---

[1] Argall. on his fishing trip, has been credited with attacking not only the French in Acadia but the Dutch traders on Manhattan. But there are grounds for doubt if he did the latter.

and Francisco Lembri an English pilot, who by my orders went to reconnoitre those ports." Small wonder that Dale was apprehensive. "What may be the daunger of this unto us," he wrote home, "who are here so few, so weake, and unfortified, . . . I refer me to your owne honorable knowledg."

Months pass, and the English Ambassador to Spain writes from Madrid that he "is not hasty to advertise anything upon bare rumours, which hath made me hitherto forbeare to write what I had generally heard of their intents against Virginia, but now I have been . . . advertised that without question they will speedily attempt against our plantation there. And that it is a thing resolved of, that ye King of Spain must run any hazard with England rather than permit ye English to settle there. . . . Whatsoever is attempted, I conceive will be from ye Havana."

Rumors fly back and forth. The next year — 1613 — the Ambassador writes from Madrid: "They have latelie had severall Consultations about our Plantation in Virginia. The resolution is — That it must be removed, but they thinke it fitt to suspend the execution of it, . . . for that they are in hope that it will fall of itselfe."

The Spanish hope seemed, at this time, not at

all without foundation. Members of the Virginia
Company had formed the Somers Islands Company — named for Somers the Admiral — and had
planted a small colony in Bermuda where the *Sea
Adventure* had been wrecked. Here were fair,
fertile islands without Indians, and without the
diseases that seemed to rise, no man knew how,
from the marshes along those lower reaches of the
great river James in Virginia. Young though it
was, the new plantation "prospereth better than
that of Virginia, and giveth greater incouragement
to prosecute yt." In England there arose, from
some concerned, the cry to "Give up Virginia
that has proved a project awry! As Gates was
once about to remove thence every living man, so
truly they might be now removed to these more
hopeful islands!" The Spanish Ambassador is
found writing to the Spanish King: "Thus they
are here discouraged . . . on account of the heavy
expenses they have incurred, and the disappoint-
ment, that there is no passage from there to the
South Sea . . . nor mines of gold or silver."
This, be it noted, was before tobacco was discovered to be an economic treasure.

The *Elizabeth* from London reached Virginia in
May, 1613. It brought to the colony news of

Bermuda, and incidentally of that new notion brewing in the mind of some of the Company. When the *Elizabeth*, after a month in Virginia, turned homeward, she carried a vigorous letter from Dale, the High Marshal, to Sir Thomas Smith, Treasurer of the Company.

Let me tell you all at home [writes Dale] this one thing, and I pray remember it; if you give over this country and loose it, you, with your wisdoms, will leap such a gudgeon as our state hath not done the like since they lost the Kingdom of France; be not gulled with the clamorous report of base people; believe Caleb and Joshua; if the glory of God have no power with them and the conversion of these poor infidels, yet let the rich mammons' desire egge them on to inhabit these countries. I protest to you, by the faith of an honest man, the more I range the country the more I admire it. I have seen the best countries in Europe; I protest to you, before the Living God, put them all together, this country will be equivalent unto them if it be inhabited with good people.

If ever Mother England seriously thought of moving Virginia into Bermuda, the idea was now given over. Spain, suspending the sword until Virginia "will fall of itselfe," saw that sword rust away.

Five years in all Dale ruled Virginia. Then.

personal and family matters calling, he sailed away home to England, to return no more. Soon his star "having shined in the Westerne, was set in the Easterne India." At the helm in Virginia he left George Yeardley, an honest, able man. But in England, what was known as the "court party" in the Company managed to have chosen instead for De La Warr's deputy governor, Captain Samuel Argall. It proved an unfortunate choice. Argall, a capable and daring buccaneer, fastened on Virginia as on a Spanish galleon. For a year he ruled in his own interest, plundering and terrorizing. At last the outcry against him grew so loud that it had to be listened to across the Atlantic. Lord De La Warr was sent out in person to deal with matters but died on the way; and Captain Yeardley, now knighted and appointed Governor, was instructed to proceed against the incorrigible Argall. But Argall had already departed to face his accusers in England.

CHAPTER VII

THE choice of Sir Edwyn Sandys as Treasurer of the Virginia Company in 1619 marks a turning-point in the history of both Company and colony. At a moment when James I was aiming at absolute monarchy and was menacing Parliament, Sandys and his party — the Liberals of the day — turned the sessions of the Company into a parliament where momentous questions of state and colonial policy were freely debated. The liberal spirit of Sandys cast a beam of light, too, across the Atlantic. When Governor Yeardley stepped ashore at Jamestown in mid-April, he brought with him, as the first fruits of the new régime, no less a boon than the grant of a representative assembly.

There were to be in Virginia, subject to the Company, subject in its turn to the Crown, two "Supreme Councils," one of which was to consist of the Governor and his councilors chosen by the Company in England. The other was to be elected by the colonists, two representatives or burgesses from each distinct settlement. Council and House of Burgesses were to constitute the upper and lower houses of the General Assembly. The whole had power to legislate upon Virginian affairs within the bounds of the colony, but the Governor in Virginia and the Company in England must approve its acts.

A mighty hope in small was here! Hedged about with provisions, curtailed and limited, here nevertheless was an acorn out of which, by natural growth and some mutation, was to come popular government wide and deep. The planting of this small seed of freedom here, in 1619, upon the banks of the James in Virginia, is an event of prime importance.

On the 30th of July, 1619, there was convened in the log church in Jamestown the first true Parliament or Legislative Assembly in America. Twenty-two burgesses sat, hat on head, in the body of the church, with the Governor and the Council in the best seats. Master John Pory, the speaker, faced the Assembly; clerk and sergeant-at-arms were at hand; Master Buck, the Jamestown minister, made the solemn opening prayer. The political divisions of this Virginia were Cities, Plantations, and Hundreds, the English population numbering now at least a thousand souls. Boroughs sending burgesses were James City, Charles City, the City of Henricus, Kecoughtan, Smith's Hundred, Flowerdieu Hundred, Martin's Hundred, Martin Brandon, Ward's Plantation, Lawne's Plantation, and Argall's Gift. This first Assembly attended to Indian questions, agriculture, and religion.

Most notable is this year 1619, a year wrought of gold and iron. John Rolfe, back in Virginia, though without his Indian princess, who now lies in English earth, jots down and makes no comment upon what he has written: "About the last of August came in a Dutch man of warre that sold us twenty Negars."

No European state of that day, few individuals, disapproved of the African slave trade. That dark continent made a general hunting-ground. England, Spain, France, the Netherlands, captured, bought, and sold slaves. Englishmen in Virginia bought without qualm, as Englishmen in England bought without qualm. The cargo of the Dutch ship was a commonplace. The only novelty was that it was the first shipload of Africans brought to English-America. Here, by the same waters, were the beginnings of popular government and the young upas-tree of slavery. A contradiction in terms was set to resolve itself, a riddle for unborn generations of Americans.

Presently there happened another importation. Virginia, under the new management, had strongly revived. Ships bringing colonists were coming in; hamlets were building; fields were being planted; up and down were to be found churches; a college at Henricus was projected so that Indian children might be taught and converted from "heathennesse." Yet was the population almost wholly a doublet-and-breeches-wearing population. The children for whom the school was building were Indian children. The men sailing to Virginia dreamed of a few years there and gathered wealth, and then return to England.

Apparently it was the new Treasurer, Sir Edwyn Sandys, who first grasped the essential principle of successful colonization: Virginia must be *home* to those we send! Wife and children made home. Sandys gathered ninety women, poor maidens and widows, "young, handsome, and chaste," who were willing to emigrate and in Virginia become wives of settlers. They sailed; their passage money was paid by the men of their choice; they married — and home life began in Virginia. In due course of time appeared fair-haired children, blue or gray of eye, with all England behind them, yet native-born, Virginians from the cradle.

Colonists in number sailed now from England. Most ranks of society and most professions were represented. Many brought education, means, independent position. Other honest men, chiefly young men with little in the purse, came over under indentures, bound for a specified term of years to settlers of larger means. These indentured men are numerous; and when they have worked out their indebtedness they will take up land of their own.

An old suggestion of Dale's now for the first time bore fruit. Over the protest of the "country party" in the Company, there began to be sent each year out of the King's gaols a number, though not at any time a large number, of men under conviction for various crimes. This practice continued, or at intervals was resumed, for years, but its consequences were not so dire, perhaps, as we might imagine. The penal laws were execrably brutal, and in the drag-net of the law might be found many merely unfortunate, many perhaps finer than the law.

Virginia thus was founded and established. An English people moved through her forests, crossed in boats her shining waters, trod the lanes of hamlets builded of wood but after English fashions. Climate, surrounding nature, differed from old England, and these and circumstance would work for variation. But the stock was Middlesex, Surrey, Devon, and all the other shires of England. Scotchmen came also, Welshmen, and, perhaps as early as this, a few Irish. And there were De La Warr's handful of Poles and Germans, and several French vine-dressers.

Political and economic life was taking form. That huge, luxurious, thick-leafed, yellow-flowered crop, alike comforting and extravagant, that tobacco that was in much to mould manners and customs and ways of looking at things, was beginning to grow abundantly. In 1620 forty thousand pounds of tobacco went from Virginia to England; two years later went sixty thousand pounds. The best sold at two shillings the pound, the inferior for eighteen pence. The Virginians dropped all thought of sassafras and clapboard. Tobacco only had any flavor of Golconda.

At this time the rich soil, composed of layer on layer of the decay of forests that had lived from old time, was incredibly fertile. As fast as trees could be felled and dragged away, in went the tobacco. Fields must have laborers, nor did these need to be especially intelligent. Bring in indentured men to work. Presently dream that ships, English as well as Dutch, might oftener load in Africa and sell in Virginia, to furnish the dark fields with dark workers! In Dale's time had begun the making over of land in fee simple; in Yeardley's time every "ancient" colonist — that is every man who had come to Virginia before 1616 — was given a goodly number of acres subject to a quit-rent. Men of means and influence obtained great holdings; ownership, rental, sale, and purchase of the land began in Virginia much as in older times it had begun in England. Only here, in America, where it seemed that the land could never be exhausted, individual holdings were often of great acreage. Thus arose the Virginia Planter.

In Yeardley's time John Berkeley established at Falling Creek the first iron works ever set up in

English-America. There were by this time in Virginia glass works, a windmill, iron works. To till the soil remained the chief industry, but the tobacco culture grew until it overshadowed the maize and wheat, the pease and beans. There were cattle and swine, not a few horses, poultry, pigeons, and peacocks.

In 1621 Yeardley, desiring to be relieved, was succeeded by Sir Francis Wyatt. In October the new Governor came from England in the *George*, and with him a goodly company. Among others is found George Sandys, brother of Sir Edwyn. This gentleman and scholar, beneath Virginia skies and with Virginia trees and blossoms about him, translated the *Metamorphoses* of Ovid and the First Book of the *Æneid*, both of which were published in London in 1626. He stands as the first purely literary man of the English New World. But vigorous enough literature, though the writers thereof regarded it as information only, had, from the first years, emanated from Virginia. Smith's *True Relation*, George Percy's *Discourse*, Strachey's *True Repertory of the Wracke and Redemption of Sir Thomas Gates*, and his *Historie of Travaile into Virginia Brittannia*, Hamor's *True Discourse*, Whitaker's *Good News* — other letters and reports

—had already flowered, all with something of the strength and fragrance of Elizabethan and early Jacobean work.

For some years there had seemed peace with the Indians. Doubtless members of the one race may have marauded, and members of the other showed themselves highhanded, impatient, and unjust, but the majority on each side appeared to have settled into a kind of amity. Indians came singly or in parties from their villages to the white men's settlements, where they traded corn and venison and what not for the magic things the white man owned. A number had obtained the white man's firearms, unwisely sold or given. The red seemed reconciled to the white's presence in the land; the Indian village and the Indian tribal economy rested beside the English settlement, church, and laws. Doubtless a fragment of the population of England and a fragment of the English in Virginia saw in a pearly dream the red man baptized, clothed, become Christian and English. At the least, it seemed that friendliness and peace might continue.

In the spring of 1622 a concerted Indian attack and massacre fell like a bolt from the blue. Up and down the James and upon the Chesapeake, everywhere on the same day, Indians, bursting from the dark forest that was so close behind every cluster of log houses, attacked the colonists. Three hundred and forty-seven English men, women, and children were slain. But Jamestown and the plantations in its neighborhood were warned in time. The English rallied, gathered force, turned upon and beat back to the forest the Indian, who was now and for a long time to come their open foe.

There followed upon this horror not a day or a month but years of organized retaliation and systematic harrying. In the end the great majority of the Indians either fell or were pushed back toward the upper Pamunkey, the Rappahannock, the Potomac, and westward upon the great shelf or terrace of the earth that climbed to the fabled mountains. And with this westward move there passed away that old vision of wholesale Christianizing.

CHAPTER VIII

In November, 1620, there sailed into a quiet harbor on the coast of what is now Massachusetts a ship named the *Mayflower*, having on board one hundred and two English Non-conformists, men and women and with them a few children. These latest colonists held a patent from the Virginia Company and have left in writing a statement of their object: "We . . . having undertaken, for the glory of God and advancement of the Christian faith, and honor of our King and Country, a voyage to plant the first colony in the northern parts of Virginia —". The mental reservation is, of course, "where perchance we may serve God as we will!" In England there obtained in some quarters a suspicion that "they meant to make a free, popular State there." Free — Popular — Public Good! These are words that began, in the second quarter of the seventeenth century, to shine and ring.

King and people had reached the verge of a great struggle. The Virginia Company was divided, as were other groups, into factions. The court party and the country party found themselves distinctly opposed. The great, crowded meetings of the Company Sessions rang with their divisions upon policies small and large. Words and phrases, comprehensive, sonorous, heavy with the future, rose and rolled beneath the roof of their great hall. There were heard amid warm discussion: Kingdom and Colony — Spain — Netherlands — France — Church and State — Papists and Schismatics — Duties, Tithes, Excise — Petitions of Grievances — Representation — Right of Assembly. Several years earlier the King had cried, "Choose the Devil, but not Sir Edwyn Sandys!" Now he declared the Company "just a seminary to a seditious parliament!" All London resounded with the clash of parties and opinions.[1] "Last week the Earl of Warwick and the Lord Cavendish fell so foul at a Virginia . . . court that the lie passed and repassed. . . . The factions . . . are growi

---

[1] In his work on *Joint-stock Companies*, vol. II, pp. 266 ff., W. R. Scott traces the history of these acute dissensions in the Virginia Company and draws conclusions distinctly unfavorable to the management of Sandys and his party. — *Editor*.

so violent that Guelfs and Ghibellines were not more animated one against another!"

Believing that the Company's sessions foreshadowed a "seditious parliament," James Stuart set himself with obstinacy and some cunning to the Company's undoing. The court party gave the King aid, and circumstances favored the attempt. Captain Nathaniel Butler, who had once been Governor of the Somers Islands and had now returned to England by way of Virginia, published in London *The Unmasked Face of Our Colony in Virginia*, containing a savage attack upon every item of Virginian administration.

The King's Privy Council summoned the Company, or rather the "country" party, to answer these and other allegations. Southampton, Sandys, and Ferrar answered with strength and cogency. But the tide was running against them. James appointed commissioners to search out what was wrong with Virginia. Certain men were shipped to Virginia to get evidence there, as well as support from the Virginia Assembly. In this attempt they signally failed. Then to England came a Virginia member of the Virginia Council, with long letters to King and Privy Council: the Sandys–Southampton administration had done more than well

for Virginia. The letters were letters of appeal.
The colony hoped that "the Governors sent over
might not have absolute authority, but might be
restrained to the consent of the Council. . . .
But above all they made it their most humble
request that they might still retain the liberty
of their General Assemblies; than which nothing
could more conduce to the publick Satisfaction
and publick Liberty."

In London another paper, drawn by Cavendish,
was given to King and Privy Council. It answered
many accusations, and among others the statement that "the Government of the companies as it
then stood was democratical and tumultuous, and
ought therefore to be altered, and reduced into the
Hands of a few." It is of interest to hear these
men speak, in the year 1623, in an England that
was close to absolute monarchy, to a King who
with all his house stood out for personal rule.
"However, they owned that, according to his Majesty's Institution, their Government had some
Show of a democratical Form; which was nevertheless, in that Case, the most just and profitable,
and most conducive to the Ends and Effects aimed
at thereby. . . . Lastly, they observed that the
opposite Faction cried out loudly against Democ-

racy, and yet called for Oligarchy; which would, as they conceived, make the Government neither of better Form, nor more monarchical."

But the dissolution of the Virginia Company was at hand. In October, 1623, the Privy Council stated that the King had "taken into his princely Consideration the distressed State of the Colony of Virginia, occasioned, as it seemed, by the Ill Government of the Company." The remedy for the ill-management lay in the reduction of the Government into fewer hands. His Majesty had resolved therefore upon the withdrawal of the Company's charter and the substitution, "with due regard for continuing and preserving the Interest of all Adventurers and private persons whatsoever," of a new order of things. The new order proved, on examination, to be the old order of rule by the Crown. Would the Company surrender the old charter and accept a new one so modeled?

The Company, through the country party, strove to gain time. They met with a succession of arbitrary measures and were finally forced to a decision. They would not surrender their charter. Then a writ of *quo warranto* was issued; trial before the King's Bench followed; and judgment was ren-

dered against the Company in the spring term of
1624. Thus with clangor fell the famous Virginia
Company.

That was one year. The March of the next year
James Stuart, King of England, died. That young
Henry who was Prince of Wales when the *Susan
Constant*, the *Goodspeed*, and the *Discovery* sailed
past a cape and named it for him Cape Henry,
also had died. His younger brother Charles, for
whom was named that other and opposite cape,
now ascended the throne as King Charles the First
of England.

In Virginia no more General Assemblies are
held for four years. King Charles embarks upon
"personal rule." Sir Francis Wyatt, a good Governor, is retained by commission and a Council is
appointed by the King. No longer are affairs to
be conducted after a fashion "democratical and
tumultuous." Orders are transmitted from England; the Governor, assisted by the Council, will
take into cognizance purely local needs; and when
he sees some occasion he will issue a proclamation.

Wyatt, recalled finally to England; George
Yeardley again, who died in a year's time; Francis
West, that brother of Lord De La Warr and an

ancient planter — these in quick succession sit in the Governor's chair. Following them John Pott, doctor of medicine, has his short term. Then the King sends out Sir John Harvey, avaricious and arbitrary, "so haughty and furious to the Council and the best gentlemen of the country," says Beverley, "that his tyranny grew at last insupportable."

The Company previously, and now the King, had urged upon the Virginians a diversified industry and agriculture. But Englishmen in Virginia had the familiar emigrant idea of making their fortunes. They had left England; they had taken their lives in their hands; they had suffered fevers, Indian attacks, homesickness, deprivation. They had come to Virginia to get rich. Now clapboards and sassafras, pitch, tar, and pine trees for masts, were making no fortune for Virginia shippers. How could they, these few folk far off in America, compete in products of the forest with northern Europe? As to mines of gold and silver, that first rich vision had proved a disheartening mirage. "They have great hopes that the mountains are very rich, from the discovery of a silver mine made nineteen years ago, at a place about four days' journey from the falls of James river; but they have not the means of transporting the ore." So, dissatisfied with some means of livelihood and disappointed in others, the Virginians turned to tobacco.

Every year each planter grew more tobacco; every year more ships were laden. In 1628 more than five hundred thousand pounds were sent to England, for to England it must go, and not elsewhere. There it must struggle with the best Spanish, for a long time valued above the best Virginian. Finally, however, James and after him Charles, agreed to exclude the Spanish. Virginia and the Somers Islands alone might import tobacco into England. But offsetting this, customs went up ruinously; a great lump sum must go annually to the King; the leaf must enter only at the port of London; so forth and so on. Finally Charles put forth his proposal to monopolize the industry, giving Virginia tobacco the English market but limiting its production to the amount which the Government could sell advantageously. Such a policy required coöperation from the colonists. The King therefore ordered the Governor to grant a Virginia Assembly, which in turn should dutifully enter into partnership with him — upon his terms. So the Virginia Assembly thus came back into history. It made a *Humble Answere* in which, for all its humility, the King's proposal was declined. The idea of the royal monopoly faded out, and Virginia continued on its own way.

The General Assembly, having once met, seems of its own motion to have continued meeting. The next year we find it in session at Jamestown, and resolving "that we should go three severall marches upon the Indians, at three severall times of the yeare," and also "that there be an especiall care taken by all commanders and others that the people doe repaire to their churches on the Saboth day, and to see that the penalty of one pound of tobacco for every time of absence, and 50 pounds for every month's absence . . . be levyed, and the delinquents to pay the same." About this time we read: "Dr. John Pott, late Governor, indicted, arraigned, and found guilty of stealing cattle, 13 jurors, 3 whereof councellors. This day wholly spent in pleading; next day, in unnecessary disputation."

These were moving times in the little colony whose population may by now have been five thousand. Harvey, the Governor, was rapacious; the King at home, autocratic. Meanwhile, signs of change and of unrest were not wanting in Europe.

England was hastening toward revolution; in Germany the Thirty Years' War was in mid-career; France and Italy were racked by strife; over the world the peoples groaned under the strain of oppression. In science, too, there was promise of revolution. Harvey — not that Governor Harvey of Virginia, but a greater in England — was writing upon the circulation of the blood. Galileo brooded over ideas of the movement of the earth; Kepler, over celestial harmonies and solar rule. Descartes was laying the foundation of a new philosophy.

In the meantime, far across the Atlantic, bands of Virginians went out against the Indians — who might, or might not, God knows! have put in a claim to be considered among the oppressed peoples. In Virginia the fat, black, tobacco-fields, steaming under a sun like the sun of Spain, called for and got more labor and still more labor. Every little sailing ship brought white workmen — called servants — consigned, indentured, apprenticed to many-acred planters. These, in return for their passage money, must serve Laban for a term of years, but then would receive Rachel, or at least Leah, in the shape of freedom and a small holding and provision with which to begin again their individual life. If they were ambitious and energetic they might presently be able, in turn, to import labor for their own acres. As yet, in Virginia, there were few African slaves — not more perhaps than a couple of hundred. But whenever ships brought them they were greedily purchased.

In Virginia, as everywhere in time of change, there arose anomalies. Side by side persisted a romantic devotion to the King and a determination to have popular assemblies; a great sense of the rights of the white individual together with African slavery; a practical, easy-going, debonair naturalism side by side with an Established Church penalizing alike Papist, Puritan, and atheist. Even so early as this, the social tone was set that was to hold for many and many a year. The suave climate was somehow to foster alike a sense of caste and good neighborliness — class distinctions and republican ideas.

The "towns" were of the fewest and rudest — little more than small palisaded hamlets, built of frame or log, poised near the water of the river James. The genius of the land was for the plantation rather than the town. The fair and large brick or frame planter's house of a later time had not yet risen, but the system was well inaugurated that set a main or "big" house upon some fair site, with cabins clustered near it, and all surrounded, save on the river front, with far-flung acres, some planted with grain and the rest with tobacco. Up and down the river these estates were strung together by the rudest roads, mere tracks through field and wood. The cart was as yet the sole wheeled vehicle. But the Virginia planter — a horseman in England — brought over horses, bred horses, and early placed horsemanship in the catalogue of the necessary colonial virtues. At this point, however, in a land of great and lesser rivers, with a network of creeks, the boat provided the chief means of communication. Behind all, enveloping all, still spread the illimitable forest, the haunt of Indians and innumerable game.

Virginians were already preparing for an expansion to the north. There was a man in Virginia named William Claiborne. This individual — able, determined, self-reliant, energetic — had come in as a young man, with the title of surveyorgeneral for the Company, in the ship that brought Sir Francis Wyatt, just before the massacre of 1622. He had prospered and was now Secretary of the Province. He held lands, and was endowed with a bold, adventurous temper and a genius for business. In a few years he had established widespread trading relations with the Indians. He and the men whom he employed penetrated to the upper shores of Chesapeake, into the forest bordering Potomac and Susquehanna. Knives and hatchets, beads, trinkets, and colored cloth were changed for rich furs and various articles that the Indians could furnish. The skins thus gathered Claiborne shipped to London merchants, and was like to grow wealthy from what his trading brought.

Looking upon the future and contemplating barter on a princely scale, he set to work and obtained exhaustive licenses from the immediate Virginian authorities, and at last from the King himself. Under these grants, Claiborne began to provide settlements for his numerous traders. Far up the Chesapeake, a hundred miles or so from Point Comfort, he found an island that he liked, and named it Kent Island. Here for his men he built cabins with gardens around them, a mill and a church. He was far from the river James and the mass of his fellows, but he esteemed himself to be in Virginia and upon his own land. What came of Claiborne's enterprise the sequel has to show.

CHAPTER IX

MARYLAND

There now enters upon the scene in Virginia a man of middle age, not without experience in planting colonies, by name George Calvert, first Lord Baltimore. Of Flemish ancestry, born in Yorkshire, scholar at Oxford, traveler, clerk of the Privy Council, a Secretary of State under James, member of the House of Commons, member of the Virginia Company, he knew many of the ramifications of life. A man of worth and weight, he was placed by temperament and education upon the side of the court party and the Crown in the growing contest over rights. About the year 1625, under what influence is not known, he had openly professed the Roman Catholic faith — and that took courage in the seventeenth century, in England!

Some years before, Calvert had obtained from the Crown a grant of a part of Newfoundland, had named it Avalon, and had built great hopes upon its settlement. But the northern winter had worked against him. He knew, for he had resided there himself with his family in that harsh clime. "From the middle of October to the middle of May there is a sad fare of winter on all this land." He is writing to King Charles, and he goes on to say: "I have had strong temptations to leave all proceedings in plantations . . . but my inclination carrying me naturally to these kind of works . . . I am determined to commit this place to fishermen that are able to encounter storms and hard weather, and to remove myself with some forty persons to your Majesty's dominion of Virginia where, if your Majesty will please to grant me a precinct of land . . . I shall endeavour to the utmost of my power, to deserve it."

With his immediate following he thereupon does sail far southward. In October, 1629, he comes in between the capes, past Point Comfort and so up to Jamestown — to the embarrassment of that capital, as will soon be evident.

Here in Church of England Virginia was a "popish recusant!" Here was an old "court party" man, one of James's commissioners, a person of rank and prestige, known, for all his recusancy, to be in favor with the present King. Here was the

Proprietary of Avalon, guessed to be dissatisfied with his chilly holding, on the scent perhaps of balmier, easier things!

The Assembly was in session when Lord Baltimore came to Jamestown. All arrivers in Virginia must take the oath of supremacy. The Assembly proposed this to the visitor who, as Roman Catholic, could not take it, and said as much, but offered his own declaration of friendliness to the powers that were. This was declined. Debate followed, ending with a request from the Assembly that the visitor depart from Virginia. Some harshnesses of speech ensued, but hospitality and the amenities fairly saved the situation. One Thomas Tindall was pilloried for "giving my lord Baltimore the lie and threatening to knock him down." Baltimore thereupon set sail, but not, perhaps, until he had gained that knowledge of conditions which he desired.

In England he found the King willing to make him a large grant, with no less powers than had clothed him in Avalon. Territory should be taken from the old Virginia; it must be of unsettled land — Indians of course not counting. Baltimore first thought of the stretch south of the river James between Virginia and Spanish Florida — a fair land of woods and streams, of good harbors, and summer weather. But suddenly William Claiborne was found to be in London, sent there by the Virginians, with representations in his pocket. Virginia was already settled and had the intention herself of expanding to the south.

Baltimore, the King, and the Privy Council weighed the matter. Westward, the blue mountains closed the prospect. Was the South Sea just beyond their sunset slopes, or was it much farther away, over unknown lands, than the first adventurers had guessed? Either way, too rugged hardship marked the west! East rolled the ocean. North, then? It were well to step in before those Hollanders about the mouth of the Hudson should cast nets to the south. Baltimore accordingly asked for a grant north of the Potomac.

He received a huge territory, stretching over what is now Maryland, Delaware, and a part of Pennsylvania. The Potomac, from source to mouth, with a line across Chesapeake and the Eastern Shore to the ocean formed his southern frontier; his northern was the fortieth parallel, from the ocean across country to the due point above the springs of the Potomac. Over this great expanse he became "true and absolute lord and proprietary," holding fealty to England, but otherwise at liberty to rule in his own domain with every power of feudal duke or prince. The King had his allegiance, likewise a fifth part of gold or silver found within his lands. All persons going to dwell in his palatinate were to have "rights and liberties of Englishmen." But, this aside, he was lord paramount. The new country received the name *Terra Mariæ* — Maryland — for Henrietta Maria, then Queen of England.

Here was a new land and a Lord Proprietor with kingly powers. Virginians seated on the James promptly petitioned King Charles not to do them wrong by so dividing their portion of the earth. But King and Privy Council answered only that Virginia and Maryland must "assist each other on all occasions as becometh fellow-subjects." William Claiborne, indeed, continued with a determined voice to cry out that lands given to Baltimore were not, as had been claimed, unsettled, seeing that he himself had under patent a town on Kent Island and another at the mouth of the Susquehanna.

Baltimore was a reflective man, a dreamer in the good sense of the term, and religiously minded. At the height of seeming good fortune he could write:

"All things, my lord, in this world pass away. . . .
They are but lent us till God please to call for them
back again, that we may not esteem anything our
own, or set our hearts upon anything but Him
alone, who only remains forever." Like his King,
Baltimore could carry far his prerogative and privi-
lege, maintaining the while not a few degrees of
inner freedom. Like all men, here he was bound,
and here he was free.

Baltimore's desire was for "enlarging his Majesty's Empire," and at the same time to provide
in Maryland a refuge for his fellow Catholics.
These were now in England so disabled and limited
that their status might fairly be called that of a per-
secuted people. The mounting Puritanism promised no improvement. The King himself had no
fierce antagonism to the old religion, but it was
beginning to be seen that Charles and Charles's
realm were two different things. A haven should
be provided before the storm blackened further.
Baltimore thus saw put into his hands a high and
holy opportunity, and made no doubt that it was
God-given. His charter, indeed, seemed to contem-
plate an established church, for it gave to Baltimore the patronage of all churches and chapels
which were to be "consecrated according to the

ecclesiastical laws of our kingdom of England";
nevertheless, no interpretation of the charter
was to be made prejudicial to "God's holy and
true Christian religion." What was Christian and
what was prejudicial was, fortunately for him, left
undefined. No obstacles were placed before a Catholic emigration.

Baltimore had this idea and perhaps a still wider
one: a land — Mary's land — where all Christians
might foregather, brothers and sisters in one
home! Religious tolerance — practical separation of
Church and State — that was a broad idea for his
age, a generous idea for a Roman Catholic of a time
not so far removed from the mediæval. True,
wherever he went and whatever might be his own
thought and feeling, he would still have for overlord
a Protestant sovereign, and the words of his charter
forbade him to make laws repugnant to the laws
of England. But Maryland was distant, and wise
management might do much. Catholics, Angli-
cans, Puritans, Dissidents, and Non-conformists of
almost any physiognomy, might come and be at
home, unpunished for variations in belief.

Only the personal friendship of England's King
and the tact and suave sagacity of the Proprietary
himself could have procured the signing of this

charter, since it was known — as it was to all who cared to busy themselves with the matter — that here was a Catholic meaning to take other Catholics, together with other scarcely less abominable sectaries, out of the reach of Recusancy Acts and religious pains and penalties, to set them free in England-in-America; and, raising there a state on the novel basis of free religion, perhaps to convert the heathen to all manner of errors, and embark on mischiefs far too large for definition. Taking things as they were in the world, remembering acts of the Catholic Church in the not distant past, the ill-disposed might find some color for the agitation which presently did arise. Baltimore was known to be in correspondence with English Jesuits, and it soon appeared that Jesuit priests were to accompany the first colonists. At that time the Society of Jesus loomed large both politically and educationally. Many may have thought that there threatened a Rome in America. But, however that may have been, there was small chance for any successful opposition to the charter, since Parliament had been dissolved by the King, not to be summoned again for eleven years. The Privy Council was subservient, and, as the Sovereign was his friend, Baltimore saw the signing of the charter assured and began to gather together his first colonists. Then, somewhat suddenly, in April, 1632, he sickened, and died at the age of fifty-three.

His son, Cecil Calvert, second Lord Baltimore, took up his father's work. This young man, likewise able and sagacious, and at every step in his father's confidence, could and did proceed even in detail according to what had been planned. All his father's rights had descended to him; in Maryland he was Proprietary with as ample power as ever a Count Palatine had enjoyed. He took up the advantage and the burden.

The father's idea had been to go with his colonists to Maryland, and this it seems that the son also meant to do. But now, in London, there deepened a clamor against such Catholic enterprise. Once he were away, lips would be at the King's ear. And with England so restless, in a turmoil of new thought, it might even arise that King and Privy Council would find trouble in acting after their will, good though that might be. The second Baltimore therefore remained in England to safeguard his charter and his interests.

The family of Baltimore was an able one. Cecil Calvert had two brothers, Leonard and George, and these would go to Maryland in his place. Leonard he made Governor and Lieutenant-general, and appointed him councilor. Ships were made ready — the *Ark* of three hundred tons and the *Dove* of fifty. The colonists went aboard at Gravesend, where these ships rode at anchor. Of the company a great number were Protestants, willing to take land, if their condition were bettered so, with Catholics. Difficulties of many kinds kept them all long at the mouth of the Thames, but at last, late in November, 1633, the *Ark* and the *Dove* set sail. Touching at the Isle of Wight, they took aboard two Jesuit priests, Father White and Father Altham, and a number of other colonists. Baltimore reported that the expedition consisted of "two of my brothers with very near twenty other gentlemen of very good fashion, and three hundred labouring men well provided in all things."

These ships, with the first Marylanders, went by the old West Indies sea route. We find them resting at Barbados; then they swung to the north and, in February, 1634, came to Point Comfort in Virginia. Here they took supplies, being treated by Sir John Harvey (who had received a letter from the King) with "courtesy and humanity." Without long tarrying, for they were sick now for land of their own, they sailed on up the great bay, the Chesapeake.

Soon they reached the mouth of the Potomac — a river much greater than any of them, save shipmasters and mariners, had ever seen — and into this turned the *Ark* and the *Dove*. After a few leagues of sailing up the wide stream, they came upon an islet covered with trees, leafless, for spring had hardly broken. The ships dropped anchor; the boats were lowered; the people went ashore. Here the Calverts claimed Maryland "for our Savior and for our Sovereign Lord the King of England," and here they heard Mass. St. Clement's they called the island.

But it was too small for a home. The *Ark* was left at anchor, while Leonard Calvert went exploring with the *Dove*. Up the Potomac some distance he went, but at the last he wisely determined to choose for their first town a site nearer the sea. The *Dove* turned and came back to the *Ark*, and both sailed on down the stream from St. Clement's Isle. Before long they came to the mouth of a tributary stream flowing in from the north. The *Dove*, going forth again, entered this river, which presently the party named the River St. George.

Soon they came to a high bank with trees tinged
with the foliage of advancing spring. Here upon
this bank the English found an Indian village
and a small Algonquin group, in the course of
extinction by their formidable Iroquois neighbors, the giant Susquehannocks. The white men
landed, bearing a store of hatchets, gewgaws, and
colored cloth. The first Lord Baltimore, having
had opportunity enough for observing savages,
had probably handed on to his sagacious sons his
conclusions as to ways of dealing with the natives
of the forest. And the undeniable logic of events
was at last teaching the English how to colonize.
Englishmen on Roanoke Island, Englishmen on
the banks of the James, Englishmen in that first
New England colony, had borne the weight of
early inexperience and all the catalogue of woes
that follow ignorance. All these early colonists
alike had been quickly entangled in strife with the
people whom they found in the land.

> First they fell on their knees,
> And then on the Aborigines.

But by now much water had passed the mill. The
thinking kind, the wiser sort, might perceive more
things than one, and among these the fact that

savages had a sense of justice and would even fight against injustice, real or fancied.

The Calverts, through their interpreter, conferred with the inhabitants of this Indian village. Would they sell lands where the white men might peaceably settle, under their given word to deal in friendly wise with the red men? Many hatchets and axes and much cloth would be given in return.

To a sylvan people store of hatchets and axes had a value beyond many fields of the boundless earth. The *Dove* appeared before them, too, at the psychological moment. They had just discussed removing, bag and baggage, from the proximity of the Iroquois. In the end, these Indians sold to the English their village huts, their cleared and planted fields, and miles of surrounding forest. Moreover they stayed long enough in friendship with the newcomers to teach them many things of value. Then they departed, leaving with the English a clear title to as much land as they could handle, at least for some time to come. Later, with other Indians, as with these, the Calverts pursued a conciliatory policy. They were aided by the fact that the Susquehannocks to the north, who might have given trouble, were involved in war with yet more northerly tribes, and could pay scant attention to the incoming white men. But even so, the Calverts proved, as William Penn proved later, that men may live at peace with men, honestly and honorably, even though hue of skin and plane of development differ.

Now the *Ark* joins the *Dove* in the River St. George. The pieces of ordnance are fired; the colonists disembark; and on the 27th of March, 1634, the Indian village, now English, becomes St. Mary's.

On the whole how advantageously are they placed! There is peace with the Indians. Huts, lodges, are already built, fields already cleared or planted. The site is high and healthful. They have at first few dissensions among themselves. Nor are they entirely alone or isolated in the New World. There is a New England to the north of them and a Virginia to the south. From the one they get in the autumn salted fish, from the other store of swine and cattle. Famine and pestilence are far from them. They build a "fort" and perhaps a stockade, but there are none of the stealthy deaths given by arrow and tomahawk in the north, nor are there any of the Spanish alarms that terrified the south. From the first they have with them women and children. They know that their settlement is "home." Soon other ships and colonists follow the *Ark* and the *Dove* to St. Mary's, and the history of this middle colony is well begun.

In Virginia, meantime, there was jealousy enough of the new colony, taking as it did territory held to be Virginian and renaming it, not for the old, independent, Protestant, virgin queen, but for a French, Catholic, queen consort — even settling it with believers in the Mass and bringing in Jesuits! It was, says a Jamestown settler, "accounted a crime almost as heinous as treason to favour, nay to speak well of that colony." Beside the Virginian folk as a whole, one man, in particular, William Claiborne, nursed an individual grievance. He had it from Governor Calvert that he might dwell on in Kent Island, trading from there, but only under license from the Lord Proprietor and as an inhabitant of Maryland, not of Virginia. Claiborne, with the Assembly at Jamestown secretly on his side, resisted this interference with his rights, and, as he continued to trade with a high hand, he soon fell under suspicion of stirring up the Indians against the Marylanders.

At the time, this quarrel rang loud through Maryland and Virginia, and even echoed across the Atlantic. Leonard Calvert had a trading-boat of Claiborne's seized in the Patuxent River. Thereupon Claiborne's men, with the shallop *Cockatrice*, in retaliation attacked Maryland pinnaces and lost both their lives and their boat. For several years Maryland and Kent Island continued intermittently to make petty war on each other. At last, in 1638, Calvert took the island by main force and hanged for piracy a captain of Claiborne's. The Maryland Assembly brought the trader under a Bill of Attainder; and a little later, in England, the Lords Commissioners of Foreign Plantations formally awarded Kent Island to the Lord Proprietor. Thus defeated, Claiborne, nursing his wrath, moved down the bay to Virginia.

CHAPTER X

CHURCH AND KINGDOM

VIRGINIA, all this time, with Maryland a thorn in her side, was wrestling with an autocratic governor, John Harvey. This avaricious tyrant sowed the wind until in 1635 he was like to reap the whirlwind. Though he was the King's Governor and in good odor in England, where rested the overpower to which Virginia must bow, yet in this year Virginia blew upon her courage until it was glowing and laid rude hands upon him. We read: "An Assembly to be called to receive complaints against Sr. John Harvey, on the petition of many inhabitants, to meet 7th of May." But, before that month was come, the Council, seizing opportunity, acted for the whole. Immediately below the entry above quoted appears: "On the 28th of April, 1635, Sr. John Harvey thrust out of his government, and Capt. John West acts as Governor till the King's pleasure known."[1]

[1] Hening's *Statutes*, vol. I, p. 223.

So Virginia began her course as rebel against political evils! It is of interest to note that Nicholas Martian, one of the men found active against the Governor, was an ancestor of George Washington.

Harvey, thrust out, took first ship for England, and there also sailed commissioners from the Virginia Assembly with a declaration of wrongs for the King's ear. But when they came to England, they found that the King's ear was for the Governor whom he had given to the Virginians and whom they, with audacious disobedience, had deposed. Back should go Sir John Harvey, still governing Virginia; back without audience the so-called commissioners, happy to escape a merited hanging! Again to Jamestown sailed Harvey. In silence Virginia received him, and while he remained Governor no Assembly sat.

But having asserted his authority, the King in a few years' time was willing to recall his unwelcome representative. So in 1639 Governor Harvey vanishes from the scene, and in comes the well-liked Sir Francis Wyatt as Governor for the second time. For two years he remains, and is then superseded by Sir William Berkeley, a notable figure in Virginia for many years to come.

The population was now perhaps ten thousand, both English born and Virginians born of English parents. A few hundred negroes moved in the tobacco fields. More would be brought in and yet more. And now above a million pounds of tobacco were going annually to England.

The century was predominantly one of inner and outer religious conflict. What went on at home in England reëchoed in Virginia. The new Governor was a dyed-in-the-wool Cavalier, utterly stubborn for King and Church. The Assemblies likewise leaned that way, as presumably did the mass of the people. It was ordered in 1631: "That there bee a uniformitie throughout this colony both in substance and circumstance to the cannons and constitutions of the church of England as neere as may bee, and that every person yeald readie obedience unto them uppon penaltie of the paynes and forfeitures in that case appoynted." And, indeed, the pains and forfeitures threatened were savage enough.

Official Virginia, loyal to the Established Church, was jealous and fearful of Papistry and looked askance at Puritanism. It frowned upon these and upon agnosticisms, atheisms, pantheisms, religious doubts, and alterations in judgment — upon anything, in short, that seemed to push a finger against Church and Kingdom. Yet in this Virginia, governed by Sir William Berkeley, a gentleman more cavalier than the Cavaliers, more royalist than the King, more churchly than the Church, there lived not a few Puritans and Dissidents, going on as best they might with Established Church and fiery King's men. Certain parishes were predominantly Puritan; certain ministers were known to have leanings away from surplices and genuflections and to hold that Archbishop Laud was some kin to the Pope. In 1642, to reënforce these ministers, came three more from New England, actively averse to conformity. But Governor and Council and the majority of the Burgesses will have none of that. The Assembly of 1643 takes sharp action.

For the preservation of the puritie of doctrine and unitie of the church, *It is enacted* that all ministers whatsoever which shall reside in the collony are to be conformable to the orders and constitutions of the church of England, and the laws therein established, and not otherwise to be admitted to teach or preach publickly or privately. And that the Gov. and Counsel do take care that all nonconformists upon notice of them shall be compelled to depart the collony with all conveniencie.

And so in consequence out of Virginia, to New England where Independents were welcome, or to Maryland where any Christian might dwell, went these tainted ministers. But there stayed behind Puritan and nonconforming minds in the bodies of many parishioners. They must hold their tongues, indeed, and outwardly conform — but they watched lynx-eyed for their opportunity and a more favorable fortune.

Having launched thunderbolts against schismatics of this sort, Berkeley, himself active and powerful, with the Council almost wholly of his party and the House of Burgesses dominantly so, turned his attention to "popish recusants." Of these there were few or none dwelling in Virginia. Let them then not attempt to come from Maryland! The rulers of the colony legislated with vigor: papists may not hold any public place; all statutes against them shall be duly executed; popish priests by chance or intent arriving within the bounds of Virginia shall be given five days' warning, and, if at the end of this time they are yet upon Virginian soil, action shall be brought against them. Berkeley sweeps with an impatient broom.

The Kingdom is cared for not less than the

Church in Virginia. Any and all persons coming into the colony by land and by sea shall have administered to them the Oath of Supremacy and Allegiance. "Which if any shall refuse to take," the commander of the fort at Point Comfort shall "committ him or them to prison." Foreigners in birth and tongue, foreigners in thought, must have found the place and time narrow indeed.

On the eve of civil war there arose on the part of some in England a project to revive and restore the old Virginia Company by procuring from Charles, now deep in troubles of his own, a renewal of the old letters patent and the transference of the direct government of the colony into the hands of a reorganized and vast corporation. Virginia, which a score of years before had defended the Company, now protested vigorously, and, with regard to the long view of things, it may be thought wisely. The project died a natural death. The petition sent from Virginia shows plainly enough the pen of Berkeley. There are a multitude of reasons why Virginia should not pass from King to Company, among which these are worthy of note: "We may not admit of so unnatural a distance as a Company will interpose between his sacred majesty and us his subjects from whose immediate protection we have received so many royal favours and gracious blessings. For, by such admissions, we shall degenerate from the condition of our birth, being naturalized under a monarchical government and not a popular and tumultuary government depending upon the greatest number of votes of persons of several humours and dispositions."

When this paper reached England, it came to a country at civil war. The Long Parliament was in session. Stafford had been beheaded, the Star Chamber swept away, the Grand Remonstrance presented. On Edgehill bloomed flowers that would soon be trampled by Rupert's cavalry. In Virginia the Assembly took notice of these "unkind differences now in England," and provided by tithing for the Governor's pension and allowance, which were for the present suspended and endangered by the troubles at home. That the forces banded against the Lord's anointed would prove victorious must at this time have appeared preposterously unlikely to the fiery Governor and the ultra-loyal Virginia whom he led. The Puritans and Independents in Virginia — estimated a little earlier at "a thousand strong" and now, for all the acts against them, probably stronger yet — were to be found chiefly in the parishes of Isle of Wight and Nansemond, but had representatives from the Falls to the Eastern Shore. What these Virginians thought of the "unkind differences" does not appear in the record, but probably there was thought enough and secret hopes.

In 1644, the year of Marston Moor, Virginia, too, saw battle and sudden and bloody death. That Opechancanough who had succeeded Powhatan was now one hundred years old, hardly able to walk or to see, dwelling harmlessly in a village upon the upper Pamunkey. All the Indians were broken and dispersed; serious danger was not to be thought of. Then, of a sudden, the flame leaped again. There fell from the blue sky a massacre directed against the outlying plantations. Three hundred men, women, and children were killed by the Indians. With fury the white men attacked in return. They sent bodies of horse into the untouched western forests. They chased and slew without mercy. In 1646 Opechancanough, brought a prisoner to Jamestown, ended his long tale of years by a shot from one of his keepers. The Indians were beaten, and, lacking such another leader, made no more organized and general attacks.

But for long years a kind of border warfare still went on.

Even Maryland, tolerant and just as was the Calvert policy, did not altogether escape Indian troubles. She had to contend with no such able chief as Opechancanough, and she suffered no sweeping massacres. But after the first idyllic year or so there set in a small, constant friction. So fast did the Maryland colonists arrive that soon there was pressure of population beyond those first purchased bounds. The more thoughtful among the Indians may well have taken alarm lest their villages and hunting-grounds might not endure these inroads. Ere long the English in Maryland were placing "centinells" over fields where men worked, and providing penalties for those who sold the savages firearms. But at no time did young Maryland suffer the Indian woes that had vexed young Virginia.

Nor did Maryland escape the clash of interests which beset the beginnings of representative assemblies in all proprietary provinces. The second, like the first, Lord Baltimore, was a believer in kings and aristocracies, in a natural division of human society into masters and men. His effort was to plant intact in Maryland a feudal order. He would be Palatine, the King his suzerain. In Maryland the great planters, in effect his barons, should live upon estates, manorial in size and with manorial rights. The laboring men — the impecunious adventurers whom these greater adventurers brought out — would form a tenantry, the Lord Proprietary's men's men. It is true that, according to charter, provision was made for an Assembly. Here were to sit "freemen of the province," that is to say, all white males who were not in the position of indentured servants. But with the Proprietary, and not with the Assembly, would rest primarily the law-making power. The Lord Proprietary would propose legislation, and the freemen of the country would debate, in a measure advise, represent, act as consultants, and finally confirm. Baltimore was prepared to be a benevolent lord, wise, fatherly.

In 1635 met the first Assembly, Leonard Calvert and his Council sitting with the burgesses, and this gathering of freemen proceeded to inaugurate legislation. There was passed a string of enactments which presumably dealt with immediate wants at St. Mary's, and which, the Assembly recognized, must have the Lord Proprietary's as-

sent. A copy was therefore sent by the first ship
to leave. So long were the voyages and so slow
the procedure in England that it was 1637 before
Baltimore's veto upon the Assembly's laws reached
Maryland. It would seem that he did not dis-
approve so much of the laws themselves as of the
bold initiative of the Assembly, for he at once sent
over twelve bills of his own drafting. Leonard
Calvert was instructed to bring all freemen together in Assembly and present for their accept-
ance the substituted legislation.

Early in 1638 this Maryland Assembly met.
The Governor put before it for adoption the Proprietary's laws. The vote was taken. Governor
and some others were for, the remainder of the
Assembly unanimously against, the proposed legislation. There followed a year or two of struggle
over this question, but in the end the Proprietary
in effect acknowledged defeat. The colonists,
through their Assembly, might thereafter propose
laws to meet their exigencies, and Governor Calvert, acting for his brother, should approve or veto
according to need.

When civil war between King and Parliament
broke out in England, sentiment in Maryland as
in Virginia inclined toward the King. But that

Puritan, Non-conformist, and republican element that was in both colonies might be expected to gain if, at home in England, the Parliamentary party gained. A Royal Governor or a Lord Proprietary's Governor might alike be perplexed by the political turmoil in the mother country. Leonard Calvert felt the need of first-hand consultation with his brother. Leaving Giles Brent in his place, he sailed for England, talked there with Baltimore himself, perplexed and filled with foreboding, and returned to Maryland not greatly wiser than when he went.

Maryland was soon convulsed by disorders which in many ways reflected the unsettled conditions in England. A London ship, commanded by Richard Ingle, a Puritan and a staunch upholder of the cause of Parliament, arrived before St. Mary's, where he gave great offense by his blatant remarks about the King and Rupert, "that Prince Rogue." Though he was promptly arrested on the charge of treason, he managed to escape and soon left the loyal colony far astern.

In the meantime Leonard Calvert had come back to Maryland, where he found confusion and a growing heat and faction and side-taking of a bitter sort. To add to the turmoil, William Claiborne, among whose dominant traits was an inability to recognize defeat, was making attempts upon Kent Island. Calvert was not long at St. Mary's ere Ingle sailed in again with letters-of-marque from the Long Parliament. Ingle and his men landed and quickly found out the Protestant moiety of the colonists. There followed an actual insurrection, the Marylanders joining with Ingle and much aided by Claiborne, who now retook Kent Island. The insurgents then captured St. Mary's and forced the Governor to flee to Virginia. For two years Ingle ruled and plundered, sequestrating goods of the Proprietary's adherents, and deporting in irons Jesuit priests. At the end of this time Calvert reappeared, and behind him a troop gathered in Virginia. Now it was Ingle's turn to flee. Regaining his ship, he made sail for England, and Maryland settled down again to the ancient order. The Governor then reduced Kent Island. Claiborne, again defeated, retired to Virginia, whence he sailed for England.

In 1647 Leonard Calvert died. Until the Proprietary's will should be known, Thomas Greene acted as Governor. Over in England, Lord Baltimore stood at the parting of the ways. The King's cause had a hopeless look. Roundhead and Par-

liament were making way in a mighty tide. Balti-
more was marked for a royalist and a Catholic.
If the tide rose farther, he might lose Maryland.
A sagacious mind, he proceeded to do all that he
could, short of denying his every belief, to pla-
cate his enemies. He appointed as Governor of
Maryland William Stone, a Puritan, and into the
Council, numbering five members, he put three
Puritans. On the other hand the interests of his
Maryland Catholics must not be endangered. He
required of the new Governor not to molest any
person "professing to believe in Jesus Christ, and
in particular any Roman Catholic." In this way
he thought that, right and left, he might provide
against persecution.

Under these complex influences the Maryland
Assembly passed in 1649 an Act concerning Religion. It reveals, upon the one hand, Christen-
dom's mercilessness toward the freethinker — in
which mercilessness, whether through conviction
or policy, Baltimore acquiesced — and, on the other
hand, that aspiration toward friendship within the
Christian fold which is even yet hardly more than
a pious wish, and which in the seventeenth century could have been felt by very few. To Baltimore and the Assembly of Maryland belongs, not

the glory of inaugurating an era of wide toleration for men and women of all beliefs or disbeliefs, whether Christian or not, but the real though lesser glory of establishing entire toleration among the divisions within the Christian circle itself. According to the Act,[1]

Whatsoever person or persons within this Province and the Islands thereunto belonging, shall from henceforth blaspheme God, that is curse him, or deny our Saviour Jesus Christ to bee the sonne of God, or shall deny the holy Trinity, . . . or the Godhead of any of the said three persons of the Trinity, or the unity of the Godhead, or shall use or utter any reproachful speeches, words or language concerning the said Holy Trinity, or any of the said three persons thereof, shall be punished with death and confiscation or forfeiture of all his or her lands and goods to the Lord Proprietary and his heires. . . . Whatsoever person or persons shall from henceforth use or utter any reproachfull words, or speeches, concerning the blessed Virgin Mary, the Mother of our Saviour, or the holy Apostles or Evangelists, or any of them, shall in such case for the first offence forfeit to the said Lord Proprietary and his heires the sum of five pound sterling. . . . Whatsoever person shall henceforth upon any occasion . . . declare, call, or denominate any person or persons whatsoever inhabiting, residing, traffiqueing, trading or comerceing within this Province, or within any of the Ports, Har-

[1] *Archives of Maryland, Proceedings and Acts of the General Assembly,* vol. i, pp. 244–247.

bors, Creeks or Havens to the same belonging, an heritick, Scismatick, Idolator, puritan, Independant, Presbiterian, popish priest, Jesuite, Jesuited papist, Lutheran, Calvenist, Anabaptist, Brownist, Antinomian, Barrowist, Roundhead, Sepatist, or any other name or term in a reproachful manner relating to matter of Religion, shall for every such Offence forfeit . . . the sum of tenne shillings sterling. . . .

Whereas the inforceing of the conscience in matters of Religion hath frequently fallen out to be of dangerous Consequence in those commonwealths where it hath been practised, . . . be it therefore also by the Lord Proprietary with the advice and consent of this Assembly, ordeyned and enacted . . . that no person or persons whatsoever within this Province . . . professing to beleive in Jesus Christ, shall from henceforth bee any waies troubled, molested or discountenanced for or in respect of his or her religion nor in the free exercise thereof . . . nor anyway compelled to the beleif or exercise of any other Religion against his or her consent, soe as they be not unfaithfull to the Lord Proprietary or molest or conspire against the civill Government. . . .

CHAPTER XI

On the 30th of January, 1649, before the palace of Whitehall, Charles the First of England was beheaded. In Virginia the event fell with a shock. Even those within the colony who were Cromwell's men rather than Charles's men seem to have recoiled from this act. Presently, too, came fleeing royalists from overseas, to add their passionate voices to those of the royalists in Virginia. Many came, "nobility, clergy and gentry, men of the first rate." A thousand are said to have arrived in the year after the King's death.

In October the Virginia Assembly met. Parliament men — and now these were walking with head in the air — might regret the execution of the past January, and yet be prepared to assert that with the fall of the kingdom fell all powers and offices named and decreed by the hapless monarch. What was a passionate royalist government doing in Virginia now that England was a Commonwealth? The passionate government answered for itself in acts passed by this Assembly. With swelling words, with a tragic accent, it denounced the late happenings in England and all the Roundhead wickedness that led up to them. It proclaimed loyalty to "his sacred Majesty that now is" — that is, to Charles Stuart, afterwards Charles the Second, then a refugee on the Continent. Finally it enacted that any who defended the late proceedings, or in the least affected to question "the undoubted and inherent right of his Majesty that now is to the Collony of Virginia" should be held guilty of high treason; and that "reporters and divulgers" of rumors tending to change of government should be punished "even to severity."

Berkeley's words may be detected in these acts of the Assembly. In no great time the Cavalier Governor conferred with Colonel Henry Norwood, one of the royalist refugees to Virginia. Norwood thereupon sailed away upon a Dutch ship and came to Holland, where he found "his Majesty that now is." Here he knelt, and invited that same Majesty to visit his dominion of Virginia, and, if he liked it, there to rest, sovereign of the Virginian people. But Charles still hoped to be

sovereign in England and would not cross the seas.
He sent, however, to Sir William Berkeley a renewal of his Governor's commission, and appointed
Norwood Treasurer of Virginia, and said, doubtless, many gay and pleasant things.

In Virginia there continued to appear from England adherents of the *ancien régime*. Men, women,
and children came until to a considerable degree
the tone of society rang Cavalier. This immigra-
tion, now lighter, now heavier, continued through
a rather prolonged period. There came now to
Virginia families whose names are often met in the
later history of the land. Now Washingtons appear, with Randolphs, Carys, Skipwiths, Brod-
naxes, Tylers, Masons, Madisons, Monroes, and
many more. These persons are not without
means; they bring with them servants; they are
in high favor with Governor and Council; they
acquire large tracts of virgin land; they bring in
indentured labor; they purchase African slaves;
they cultivate tobacco. From being English country gentlemen they turn easily to become Virginia
planters.

But the Virginia Assembly had thrown a gaunt-
let before the victorious Commonwealth; and the
Long Parliament now declared the colony to be

in contumacy, assembled and dispatched ships against her, and laid an embargo upon trade with the rebellious daughter. In January of 1652 English ships appeared off Point Comfort. Four Commissioners of the Commonwealth were aboard, of whom that strong man Claiborne was one. After issuing a proclamation to quiet the fears of the people, the Commissioners made their way to Jamestown. Here was found the indomitable Berkeley and his Council in a state of active preparation, cannon trained. But, when all was said, the Commissioners had brought wisely moderate terms: submit because submit they must, acknowledge the Commonwealth, and, that done, rest unmolested! If resistance continued, there were enough Parliament men in Virginia to make an army. Indentured servants and slaves should receive freedom in exchange for support to the Commonwealth. The ships would come up from Point Comfort, and a determined war would be on. What Sir William Berkeley personally said has not survived. But after consultation upon consultation Virginia surrendered to the Commonwealth.

Berkeley stepped from the Governor's chair, retiring in wrath and bitterness of heart to his house at Greenspring. In his place sat Richard Bennett, one of the Commissioners. Claiborne was made Secretary. King's men went out of office; Parliament men came in. But there was no persecution. In the bland and wide Virginia air minds failed to come into hard and frequent collision. For all the ferocities of the statute books, acute suffering for difference of opinion, whether political or religious, did not bulk large in the life of early Virginia.

The Commissioners, after the reduction of Virginia, had a like part to play with Maryland. At St. Mary's, as at Jamestown, they demanded and at length received submission to the Commonwealth. There was here the less trouble owing to Baltimore's foresight in appointing to the office of Governor William Stone, whose opinions, political and religious, accorded with those of revolutionary England. Yet the Governor could not bring himself to forget his oath to Lord Baltimore and agree to the demand of the Commissioners that he should administer the Government in the name of "the Keepers of the Liberties of England." After some hesitation the Commissioners decided to respect his scruples and allow him to govern in the name of the Lord Proprietary, as he had solemnly promised.

In Virginia and in Maryland the Commonwealth and the Lord Protector stand where stood the Kingdom and the King. Many are far better satisfied than they were before; and the confirmed royalist consumes his grumbling in his own circle. The old, exhausting quarrel seems laid to rest. But within this wider peace breaks out suddenly an interior strife. Virginia would, if she could, have back all her old northward territory. In 1652 Bennett's Government goes so far as to petition Parliament to unseat the Catholic Proprietary of Maryland and make whole again the ancient Virginia. The hand of Claiborne, that remarkable and persistent man, may be seen in this.

In Maryland, Puritans and Independents were settled chiefly about the rivers Severn and Patuxent and in a village called Providence, afterwards Annapolis. These now saw their chance to throw off the Proprietary's rule and to come directly under that of the Commonwealth. So thinking, they put themselves into communication with Bennett and Claiborne. In 1654 Stone charged the Commissioners with having promoted "faction, sedition, and rebellion against the Lord Baltimore." The charge was well founded. Claiborne and Bennett assumed that they were yet Parliamentary Commissioners, empowered to bring "all plantations within the Bay of Chesapeake to their due obedience to the Parliament and Commonwealth of England." And they were indeed set against the Lord Baltimore. Claiborne would head the Puritans of Providence; and a troop should be raised in Virginia and march northward. The Commissioners actually advanced upon St. Mary's, and with so superior a force that Stone surrendered, and a Puritan Government was inaugurated. A Puritan Assembly met, debarring any Catholics. Presently it passed an act annulling the Proprietary's Act of Toleration. Professors of the religion of Rome should "be restrained from the exercise thereof." The hand of the law was to fall heavily upon "popery, prelacy, or licentiousness of opinion." Thus was intolerance alive again in the only land where she had seemed to die!

In England now there was hardly a Parliament, but only the Lord Protector, Oliver Cromwell. Content with Baltimore's recognition of the Protectorate, Cromwell was not prepared to back, in their independent action, the Commissioners of that now dissolved Parliament. Baltimore made sure of this, and then dispatched messengers overᴸeas to Stone, bidding him do all that lay in him to retake Maryland. Stone thereupon gathered several hundred men and a fleet of small sailing craft, with which he pushed up the bay to the Severn. In the meantime the Puritans had not been idle, but had themselves raised a body of men and had taken over the *Golden Lyon*, an armed merchantman lying before their town. On the 24th of March, 1655, the two forces met in the Battle of the Severn. "In the name of God, fall on!" cried the men of Providence, and "Hey for St. Mary's!" cried the others. The battle was won by the Providence men. They slew or wounded fifty of the St. Mary's men and desperately wounded Stone himself and took many prisoners, ten of whom were afterwards condemned to death and four were actually executed.

Now followed a period of up and down, the Commissioners and the Proprietary alike appealing to the Lord Protector for some expression of his "determinate will." Both sides received encouragement inasmuch as he decided for neither. His own authority being denied by neither, Cromwell may have preferred to hold these distant factions in a canceling, neutralizing posture. But far weightier matters, in fact, were occupying

his mind. In 1657, weary of her "very sad, dis-
tracted, and unsettled condition," Maryland herself proceeded — Puritan, Prelatist, and Catholic
together — to agree henceforth to disagree. Toleration viewed in retrospect appears dimly to have
been seen for the angel that it was. Maryland
would return to the Proprietary's rule, provided
there should be complete indemnity for political
offenses and a solemn promise that the Toleration
Act of 1649 should never be repealed. This without a smile Baltimore promised. Articles were
signed; a new Assembly composed of all manner of
Christians was called; and Maryland returned for
a time to her first allegiance.

Quiet years, on the whole, follow in Virginia
under the Commonwealth. The three Governors
of this period — Bennett, Digges, and Mathews —
are all chosen by the Assembly, which, but for
the Navigation Laws,[1] might almost forget the
Home Government. Then Oliver Cromwell dies;
and, after an interval, back to England come
the Stuarts. Charles II is proclaimed King. And
back into office in Virginia is brought that staunch

[1] See Editor's Note on the Navigation Laws at the end of this
volume.

old monarchist, Sir William Berkeley — first by a royalist Assembly and presently by commission from the new King.

Then Virginia had her Long Parliament or Assembly. In 1661, in the first gush of the Restoration, there was elected a House of Burgesses so congenial to Berkeley's mind that he wished to see it perpetuated. For fifteen years therefore he held it in being, with adjournments from one year into another and with sharp refusals to listen to any demand for new elections. Yet this demand grew, and still the Governor shut the door in the face of the people and looked imperiously forth from the window. His temper, always fiery, now burned vindictive; his zeal for King and Church and the high prerogatives of the Governor of Virginia became a consuming passion.

When Berkeley first came to Virginia, and again for a moment in the flare of the Restoration, his popularity had been real, but for long now it had dwindled. He belonged to an earlier time, and he held fast to old ideas that were decaying at the heart. A bigot for the royal power, a man of class with a contempt for the generality and its clumsily expressed needs, he grew in narrowness as he grew in years.

Berkeley could in these later times write home, though with some exaggeration: "I thank God there are no free schools nor printing, and I hope we shall not have these hundred years; for learning has brought disobedience into the world and printing has divulged them, and libels against the best governments' God keep us from both!" But that was the soured zealot for absolutism — William Berkeley the man was fond enough of books and himself had written plays.

The spirit of the time was reactionary in Virginia as it was reactionary in England. Harsh servant and slave laws were passed. A prison was to be erected in each county; provision was made for pillory and stocks and ducking-stool; the Quakers were to be proceeded against; the Baptists who refused to bring children to baptism were to suffer. Then at last in 1670 came restriction of the franchise:

Act III. *Election of Burgesses by whom.* WHEREAS the usuall way of chuseing burgesses by the votes of all persons who haveing served their tyme are freemen of this country who haveing little interest in the country doe oftener make tumults at the election to the disturbance of his Majestie's peace, than by their discretions in their votes provide for the conservation thereof, by makeing choyce of persons fitly qualifyed for the discharge of soe greate a trust, And whereas the lawes of England grant a voyce in such election only to such as by their estates real or personall have interest enough to tye them to the endeavour of the publique good; *It is hereby enacted*, that none but freeholders and housekeepers who only are answerable to the publique for the levies shall hereafter have a voice in the election of any burgesses in this country.[1]

Three years later another woe befell the colony. That same Charles II — to whom in misfortune Virginia had so adhered that for her loyalty she had received the name of the Old Dominion — now granted "all that entire tract, territory, region, and dominion of land and water commonly called Virginia, together with the territory of Accomack," to Lord Culpeper and the Earl of Arlington. For thirty-one years they were to hold it, paying to the King the slight annual rent of forty shillings. They were not to disturb the colonists in any guaranteed right of life or land or goods, but for the rest they might farm Virginia. The country cried out in anger. The Assembly hurried commissioners on board a ship in port and sent them to England to besiege the ear of the King.

Distress and discontent increased, with good reason, among the mass of the Virginians. The

[1] Hening's *Statutes*, vol. II, p. 280.

King in England, his councilors, and Parliament, played an unfatherly rôle, while in Virginia economic hardships pressed ever harder and the administration became more and more oppressive. By 1676 the gunpowder of popular indignation was laid right and left, awaiting the match.

CHAPTER XII

NATHANIEL BACON

To add to the uncertainty of life in Virginia, Indian troubles flared up again. In and around the main settlements the white man was safe enough from savage attack. But it was not so on the edge of the English world, where the white hue ran thin, where small clusters of folk and even single families built cabins of logs and made lonely clearings in the wilderness.

Not far from where now rises Washington the Susquehannocks had taken possession of an old fort. These Indians, once in league with the Iroquois but now quarreling violently with that confederacy, had been defeated and were in a mood of undiscriminating bitterness and vengeance. They began to waylay and butcher white men and women and children. In self-protection Maryland and Virginia organized in common an expedition against the Indian stronghold. In the deep woods beyond the Potomac, red men and white came to a parley. The Susquehannocks sent envoys. There was wrong on both sides. A dispute arose. The white men, waxing angry, slew the envoys — an evil deed which their own color in Maryland and in Virginia reprehended and repudiated. But the harm was done. From the Potomac to the James Indians listened to Indian eloquence, reciting the evils that from the first the white man had brought. Then the red man, in increasing numbers, fell upon the outlying settlements of the pioneers.

In Virginia there soon arose a popular clamor for effective action. Call out the militia of every county! March against the Indians! Act! But the Governor was old, of an ill temper now, and most suspicious of popular gatherings for any purpose whatsoever. He temporized, delayed, refused all appeals until the Assembly should meet.

Dislike of Berkeley and his ways and a growing sense of injury and oppression began to quiver hard in the Virginian frame. The King was no longer popular, nor Sir William Berkeley, nor were the most of the Council, nor many of the burgesses of that Long Assembly. There arose a loud demand for a new election and for changes in public policy.

Where a part of Richmond now stands, there stretched at that time a tract of fields and hills and a clear winding creek, held by a young planter named Nathaniel Bacon, an Englishman of that family which produced "the wisest, greatest, meanest of mankind." The planter himself lived farther down the river. But he had at this place an overseer and some indentured laborers. This Nathaniel Bacon was a newcomer in Virginia — a young man who had been entered in Gray's Inn, who had traveled, who was rumored to have run through much of his own estate. He had a cousin, also named Nathaniel Bacon, who had come fifteen years earlier to Virginia "a very rich, politic man and childless," and whose representations had perhaps drawn the younger Bacon to Virginia. At any rate he was here, and at the age of twenty-eight the owner of much land and the possessor of a seat in the Council. But, though he sat in the Council, he was hardly of the mind of the Governor and those who supported him.

It was in the spring of 1676 that there began a series of Indian attacks directed against the plantations and the outlying cabins of the region above the Falls of the Far West. Among the victims were men of Bacon's plantation, for his overseer and

several of his servants were slain. The news of
this massacre of his men set their young master
afire. Even a less hideous tale might have done it,
for he was of a bold and ardent nature.

Riding up the forest tracks, a company of planters from the threatened neighborhood gathered
together. "Let us make a troop and take fire and
sword among them!" There lacked a commander.
"Mr. Bacon, you command!" Very good; and
Mr. Bacon, who is a born orator, made a speech
dealing with the "grievances of the times." Very
good indeed; but still there lacked the Governor's
commission. "Send a swift messenger to Jamestown for it!"

The messenger went and returned. No commission. Mr. Bacon had made an unpleasant impression upon Sir William Berkeley. This young
man, the Governor said, was "popularly inclined"
— had "a constitution not consistent with" all
that Berkeley stood for. Bacon and his neighbors
listened with bent brows to their envoy's report. Murmurs began and deepened. "Shall we
stand idly here considering formalities, while the
redskins murder?" Commission or no commission, they would march; and in the end, march
they did — a considerable troop — to the up-river

country, with the tall, young, eloquent man at their head.

News reached the Governor at Jamestown that they were marching. In a tight-lipped rage he issued a proclamation and sent it after them. They and their leader were acting illegally, usurping military powers that belonged elsewhere! Let them disband, disperse to their dwellings, or beware action of the rightful powers! Troubled in mind, some disbanded and dispersed, but threescore at least would by no means do so. Nor would the young man "of precipitate disposition" who headed the troop. He rode on into the forest after the Indians, and the others followed him. Here were the Falls of the Far West, and here on a hill the Indians had a "fort." This the Virginia planters attacked. The hills above the James echoed to the sound of the small, desperate fray. In the end the red men were routed. Some were slain; some were taken prisoner; others escaped into the deep woods stretching westward.

In the meantime another force of horsemen had been gathered. It was headed by Berkeley and was addressed to the pursuit and apprehension of Nathaniel Bacon, who had thus defied authority. But before Berkeley could move far, fire broke out around him. The grievances of the people were many and just, and not without a family resemblance to those that precipitated the Revolution a hundred years later. Not Bacon alone, but many others who were in despair of any good under their present masters were ready for heroic measures. Berkeley found himself ringed about by a genuine popular revolt. He therefore lacked the time now to pursue Nathaniel Bacon, but spurred back to Jamestown there to deal as best he might with dangerous affairs. At Jamestown, willy-nilly, the old Governor was forced to promise reforms. The Long Assembly should be dissolved and a new Assembly, more conformable to the wishes of the people, should come into being ready to consider all their troubles. So writs went out; and there presently followed a hot and turbulent election, in which that "restricted franchise" of the Long Assembly was often defied and in part set aside. Men without property presented themselves, gave their voices, and were counted. Bacon, who had by now achieved an immense popularity, was chosen burgess for Henricus County.

In the June weather Bacon sailed down to Jamestown, with a number of those who had backed him in that assumption of power to raise troops and go against the Indians. When he came to Jamestown it was to find the high sheriff waiting for him by the Governor's orders. He was put under arrest. Hot discussion followed. But the people were for the moment in the ascendent, and Bacon should not be sacrificed. A compromise was reached. Bacon was technically guilty of "unlawful, mutinous and rebellious practises." If, on his knees before Governor, Council, and Burgesses, he would acknowledge as much and promise henceforth to be his Majesty's obedient servant, he and those implicated with him should be pardoned. He himself might be readmitted to the Council, and all in Virginia should be as it had been. He should even have the commission he had acted without to go and fight against the Indians.

Bacon thereupon made his submission upon his knees, promising that henceforth he would "demean himself dutifully, faithfully, and peaceably." Formally forgiven, he was restored to his place in the Virginia Council. An eye-witness reports that presently he saw "Mr. Bacon on his quondam seat with the Governor and Council, which seemed a marvellous indulgence to one whom he had so lately proscribed as a rebel."

The Assembly of 1676 was of a different temper and opinion from that of the Long Assembly. It was an insurgent body, composed to a large degree of mere freemen and small planters, with a few of the richer, more influential sort who nevertheless queried that old divine right of rule. Berkeley thought that he had good reason to doubt this Assembly's intentions, once it gave itself rein. He directs it therefore to confine its attention to Indian troubles. It did, indeed, legislate on Indian affairs by passing an elaborate act for the prosecution of the war. An army of a thousand white men was to be raised. Bacon was to be commander-in-chief. All manner of precautions were to be taken. But this matter disposed of, the Assembly thereupon turned to "the redressing several grievances the country was then labouring under; and motions were made for inspecting the public revenues, the collectors' accounts," and so forth. The Governor thundered; friends of the old order obstructed; but the Assembly went on its way, reforming here and reforming there. It even went so far as to repeal the preceding Assembly's legislation regarding the franchise. All white males who are freemen were now privileged to vote, "together with the freeholders and housekeepers."

A certain member wanted some detail of procedure retained because it was customary. "'Tis true it has been customary," answered another, "but if we have any bad customs amongst us, we are come here to mend 'em!" "Whereupon," says the contemporary narrator, "the house was set in a laughter." But after so considerable an amount of mending there threatened a standstill. What was to come next? Could men go further — as they had gone further in England not so many years ago? Reform had come to an apparent impasse. While it thus hesitated, the old party gained in life.

Bacon, now petitioning for his promised commission against the Indians, seems to have reached the conclusion that the Governor might promise but meant not to perform, and not only so, but that in Jamestown his very life was in danger. He had "intimation that the Governor's generosity in pardoning him and restoring him to his place in the Council were no other than previous wheedles to amuse him."

In Jamestown lived one whom a chronicler paints for us as "thoughtful Mr. Lawrence." This gentleman was an Oxford scholar, noted for "wit, learning, and sobriety . . . nicely honest, affable and without blemish in his conversation and deal-ings." Thus friends declared, though foes said of him quite other things. At any rate, having emigrated to Virginia and married there, he had presently acquired, because of a lawsuit over land in which he held himself to be unjustly and shab-bily treated through influences of the Governor, an inveterate prejudice against that ruler. He calls him in short "an old, treacherous villain." Law-rence and his wife, not being rich, kept a tavern at Jamestown, and there Bacon lodged, probably having been thrown with Lawrence before this. Persons are found who hold that Lawrence was the brain, Bacon the arm, of the discontent in Virginia. There was also Mr. William Drummond, who will be met with in the account of Carolina. He was a "sober Scotch gentleman of good repute" — but no more than Lawrence on good terms with the Governor of Virginia.

On a morning in June, when the Assembly met, it was observed that Nathaniel Bacon was not in his place in the Council — nor was he to be found in the building, nor even in Jamestown itself, though Berkeley had Lawrence's inn searched for him. He had left the town — gone up the river in his sloop to his plantation at Curles Neck "to visit his wife, who, as she informed him, was indisposed." In truth it appears that Bacon had gone for the purpose of gathering together some six hundred up-river men. Or perhaps they themselves had come together and, needing a leader, had turned naturally to the man who was under the frown of an unpopular Governor and all the Governor's supporters in Virginia. At any rate Bacon was presently seen at the head of no inconsiderable army for a colony of less than fifty thousand souls. Those with him were only up-river men; but he must have known that he could gather besides from every part of the country. Given some initial success, he might even set all Virginia ablaze. Down the river he marched, he and his six hundred, and in the summer heat entered Jamestown and drew up before the Capitol. The space in front of this building was packed with the Jamestown folk and with the six hundred. Bacon, a guard behind him, advanced to the central door, to find William Berkeley standing there shaking with rage. The old royalist has courage. He tears open his silken vest and fine shirt and faces the young man who, though trained in the law of the realm, is now filling that law with a hundred wounds.

He raises a passionate voice. "Here! Shoot me! 'Fore God, a fair mark — a fair mark! Shoot!"

Bacon will not shoot him, but will have that promised commission to go against the Indians. Those behind him lift and shake their guns. "We will have it! We will have it!" Governor and Council retire to consider the demand. If Berkeley is passionate and at times violent, so is Bacon in his own way, for an eye-witness has to say that "he displayed outrageous postures of his head, arms, body and legs, often tossing his hand from his sword to his hat," and that outside the door he had cried: "Damn my blood! I'll kill Governor, Council, Assembly and all, and then I'll sheathe my sword in my own heart's blood!" He is no dour, determined, unwordy revolutionist like the Scotch Drummond, nor still and subtle like "the thoughtful Mr. Lawrence." He is young and hot, a man of oratory and outward acts. Yet is he a patriot and intelligent upon broad public needs. When presently he makes a speech to the excited Assembly, it has for subject-matter "preserving our lives from the Indians, inspecting the public revenues, the exorbitant taxes, and redressing the grievances and calamities of that deplorable country." It has quite the ring of young men's speeches in British colonies a century later!

The Governor and his party gave in perforce. Bacon got his commission and an Act of Indemnity for all chance political offenses. General and Commander-in-chief against the Indians — so was he styled. Moreover, the Burgesses, with an alarmed thought toward England, drew up an explanatory memorial for Charles II's perusal. This paper journeyed forth upon the first ship to sail, but it had for traveling companion a letter secretly sent from the Governor to the King. The two communications were painted in opposite colors. "I have," says Berkeley, "for above thirty years governed the most flourishing country the sun ever shone over, but am now encompassed with rebellion like waters."

CHAPTER XIII

REBELLION AND CHANGE

Bacon with an increased army now rode out once more against the Indians. He made a rendezvous on the upper York — the old Pamunkey — and to this center he gathered horsemen until there may nave been with him not far from a thousand mounted men. From here he sent detachments against the red men's villages in all the upper troubled country, and afar into the sunset woods where the pioneer's cabin had not yet been builded. He acted with vigor. The Indians could not stand against his horsemen and concerted measures, and back they fell before the white men, westward again; or, if they stayed in the ever dwindling villages, they gave hostages and oaths of peace. Quiet seemed to descend once more upon the border.

But, if the frontier seemed peaceful, Virginia behind the border was a bubbling cauldron. Bacon had now become a hero of the people, a Siegfried capable of slaying the dragon. Nor were Lawrence and Drummond idle, nor others of their way of thinking. The Indian troubles might soon be settled, but why not go further, marching against other troubles, more subtle and long-continuing, and threatening all the future?

In the midst of this speculation and promise of change, the Governor, feeling the storm, dissolved the Assembly, proclaimed Bacon and his adherents rebels and traitors, and made a desperate attempt to raise an army for use against the new-fangledness of the time. This last he could not do. Private interest led many planters to side with him, and there was a fair amount of passionate conviction matching his own, that his Majesty the King and the forces of law and order were being withstood, and without just cause. But the mass of the people cried out to his speeches, "Bacon! Bacon!" As the popular leader had been warned from Jamestown by news of personal danger, so in his turn Berkeley seems to have believed that his own liberty was threatened. With suddenness he departed the place, boarded a sloop, and was "wafted over Chesapeake Bay thirty miles to Accomac."

The news of the Governor's flight, producing both alarm in one party and enthusiasm in the other, tended to precipitate the crisis. Though the Indian trouble might by now be called adjusted, Bacon, far up the York, did not disband his men. He turned and with them marched down country, not to Jamestown, but to a hamlet called Middle Plantation, where later was to grow the town of Williamsburg. Here he camped, and here took counsel with Lawrence and Drummond and others, and here addressed, with a curious, lofty eloquence, the throng that began to gather. Hence, too, he issued a "Declaration," recounting the misdeeds of those lately in power, protesting against the terms rebel and traitor as applied to himself and his followers, who are only in arms to protect his Majesty's demesne and subjects, and calling on those who are well disposed to reform to join him at Middle Plantation, there to consider the state of the country which had been brought into a bad way by "Sir William's doting and irregular actings."

Upon his proclamation many did come to Middle Plantation, great planters and small, men just freed from indentured service, holders of no land and little land and much land, men of all grades of weight and consideration and all degrees of revolutionary will, from Drummond — with a reported speech, "I am in overshoes; I will be in overboots!" and a wife Sarah who snapped a stick in two with the cry, "I care no more for the power of England than for this broken straw!" — to those who would be revolutionary as long as, and only when, it seemed safe to be so.

How much of revolution, despite that speech about his Majesty's demesne and subjects, was in Bacon's mind, or in Richard Lawrence's mind and William Drummond's mind, or in the mind of their staunchest supporters, may hardly now be resolved. Perhaps as much as was in the mind of Patrick Henry, Thomas Jefferson, and George Mason a century later.

The Governor was in Accomac, breathing fire and slaughter, though as yet without brand or sword with which to put his ardent desires into execution. But he and the constituted order were not without friends and supporters. He had, as his opponents saw, a number of "wicked and pernicious counsellors, aides and assistants against the commonalty in these our cruel commotions." Moreover — and a great moreover is that! — it was everywhere bruited that he had sent to Eng-

land, to the King, "for two thousand Red Coates."
Perhaps the King — perhaps England — will take
his view, and, not consulting the good of Virginia,
send the Red Coats! What then?

Bacon, as a measure of opposition, proposed "a
test or recognition," to be signed by those here at
Middle Plantation who earnestly do wish the good
of Virginia. It was a bold test! Not only should
they covenant to give no aid to the whilom Governor against this new general and army, but if ships
should bring the Red Coats they were to withstand
them. There is little wonder that "this bugbear
did marvellously startle" that body of Virginia
horsemen, those progressive gentlemen planters,
and others. Yet in the end, after violent contentions, the assembly at Middle Plantation drew up
and signed a remarkable paper, the "Oath at
Middle Plantation." Historically, it is linked on
the one hand with that "thrusting out of his
government" of Sir John Harvey in Charles I's
time, and on the other with Virginian proceedings
a hundred years later under the third George. If
his Majesty had been, as it was rumored, wrongly
informed that Virginia was in rebellion; if, acting
upon that misinformation, he sent troops against
his loyal Virginians — who were armed only

against an evil Governor and intolerable woes —
then these same good loyalists would "oppose and
suppress all forces whatsoever of that nature, until
such time as the King be fully informed of the
state of the case." What was to happen if the King,
being informed, still supported Berkeley and sent
other Red Coats was not taken into consideration.

This paper, being drawn, was the more quickly
signed because there arrived, in the midst of the
debate, a fresh Indian alarm. Attack threatened
a fort upon the York — whence the Governor had
seen fit to remove arms and ammunition! The
news came most opportunely for Bacon. "There
were no more discourses." The major portion of
the large assemblage signed.

The old Government in Virginia was thus denied.
But it was held that government there must be,
and that the people of Virginia through representatives must arrange for it. Writs of election, made
as usual in the King's name, and signed by Bacon
and by those members of the Council who were of
the revolt, went forth to all counties. The Assembly thus provided was to meet at Jamestown in
September.

So much business done, off rode Bacon and his
men to put down this latest rising of the Indians.

Not only these but red men in a new quarter, tribes south of the James, kept them employed for weeks to come. Nor were they unmindful of that proud old man, Sir William Berkeley, over on the Eastern Shore, a well-peopled region where traveling by boat and by sandy road was sufficiently easy. Bacon, Lawrence, and Drummond finally decided to take Sir William captive and to bring him back to Jamestown. For this purpose they dispatched a ship across the Bay, with two hundred and fifty men, under the command of Giles Bland, "a man of courage and haughty bearing," and "no great admirer of Sir William's goodness." The ship proceeded to the Accomac shore, anchored in some bight, and sent ashore men to treat with the Governor. But the Governor turned the tables on them. He made himself captor, instead of being made captive. Bland and his lieutenants were taken, whereupon their following surrendered into Berkeley's hands. Bland's second in command was hanged; Bland himself was held in irons.

Now Berkeley's star was climbing. In Accomac he gathered so many that, with those who had fled with him and later recruits who crossed the Bay, he had perhaps a thousand men. He stowed these upon the ship of the ill-fated Bland and upon a number of sloops. With seventeen sail in all, the old Governor set his face west and south towards the mouth of the James.

In that river, on the 7th of September, 1676, there appeared this fleet of the King's Governor, set on retaking Virginia. Jamestown had notice. The Bacon faction held the place with perhaps eight hundred men, Colonel Hansford at their head. Summoned by Berkeley to surrender, Hansford refused, but that same night, by advice of Lawrence and Drummond, evacuated the place, drawing his force off toward the York. The next day, emptied of all but a few citizens, Jamestown received the old Governor and his army.

The tidings found Bacon on the upper York. Acting with his accustomed energy, he sent out, far and wide, ringing appeals to the country to rouse itself, for men to join him and march to the defeat of the old tyrant. Numbers did come in. He moved with "marvelous celerity." When he had, for the time and place, a large force of rebels, he marched, by stream and plantation, tobacco-field and forest, forge and mill, through the early autumn country to Jamestown. Civil war was on.

Across the narrow neck of the Jamestown peninsula had been thrown a sort of fortification with ditch, earthwork, and palisade. Before this Bacon now sounded trumpets. No answer coming, but the mouths of cannon appearing at intervals above the breastwork, the "rebel" general halted, encamped his men, and proceeded to construct siege lines of his own. The work must be done exposed to Sir William's iron shot.

Now comes a strange and discreditable incident. Patriots, revolutionists, who on the whole would serve human progress, have yet, as have we all, dark spots and seamy sides. Bacon's parties of workmen were threatened, hindered, driven from their task by Berkeley's guns. Bacon had a curious, unadmirable idea. He sent horsemen to neighboring loyalist plantations to gather up and bring to camp, not the planters — for they are with Berkeley in Jamestown — but the planters' wives. Here are Mistress Bacon (wife of the elder Nathaniel Bacon), Mistress Bray, Mistress Ballard, Mistress Page, and others. Protesting, these ladies enter Bacon's camp, who sends one as envoy into the town with the message that, if Berkeley attacks, the whole number of women shall be placed as shield to Bacon's men who build earthworks.

He was as good — or as bad — as his word. At

the first show of action against his workmen these royalist women were placed in the front and were kept there until Bacon had made his counter-line of defense. Sir William Berkeley had great faults, but at times — not always — he displayed chivalry. For that day "the ladies' white aprons" guarded General Bacon and all his works. The next day, the defenses completed, this "white garde" was withdrawn.

Berkeley waited no longer but, though now at a disadvantage, opened fire and charged with his men through gate and over earthworks. The battle that followed was short and decisive. Berkeley's chance-gathered army was no match for Bacon's seasoned Indian fighters and for desperate men who knew that they must win or be hanged for traitors. The Governor's force wavered and, unable to stand its ground, turned and fled, leaving behind some dead and wounded. Then Bacon, who also had cannon, opened upon the town and the ships that rode before it. In the night the King's Governor embarked for the second time and with him, in that armada from the Eastern Shore, the greater part of the force he had gathered. When dawn came, Bacon saw that the ships, large and small. were gone, sailing back to Accomac.

Bacon and his following thus came peaceably into Jamestown, but with the somewhat fell determination to burn the place. It should "harbor no more rogues." What Bacon, Lawrence, Drummond, Hansford, and others really hoped — whether they forecasted a republican Virginia finally at peace and prosperous — whether they saw in a vision a new capital, perhaps at Middle Plantation, perhaps at the Falls of the Far West, a capital that should be without old, tyrannic memories — cannot now be said. However it all may be, they put torch to the old capital town and soon saw it consumed, for it was no great place, and not hard to burn.

Jamestown had hardly ceased to smoke when news came that loyalists under Colonel Brent were gathering in northern counties. Bacon, now ill but energetic to the end, turned with promptness to meet this new alarm. He crossed the York and marched northward through Gloucester County. But the rival forces did not come to a fight. Brent's men deserted by the double handful. They came into Bacon's ranks "resolving with the Persians to go and worship the rising sun." Or, hanging fire, reluctant to commit themselves either way, they melted from Brent, running homeward by

every road. Bacon, with an enlarged, not lessened
army, drew back into Gloucester. Revolutionary
fortunes shone fair in prospect. Yet it was but the
moment of brief, deceptive bloom before decay
and fall.

At this critical moment Bacon fell sick and died.
Some said that he was poisoned, but that has never
been proved. The illness that had attacked him
during his siege of Jamestown and that held on
after his victory seems to have sufficed for his
taking off. In Gloucester County he "surrendered
up that fort he was no longer able to keep, into the
hands of that grim and all-conquering Captaine
Death." His body was buried, says the old account, "but where deposited till the Generall day
not knowne, only to those who are resolutely silent
in that particular."

With Bacon's death there fell to pieces all this
hopeful or unhopeful movement. Lawrence might
have a subtle head and Drummond the courage
to persevere; Hansford, Cheeseman, Bland, and
others might have varied abilities. But the passionate and determined Bacon had been the organ
of action; Bacon's the eloquence that could bring to
the cause men with property to give as well as men
with life to lose. It is a question how soon, had

Bacon not died, must have failed his attempt at revolution, desperate because so premature.

Back came Berkeley from Accomac, his turbulent enemy thus removed. All who from the first had held with the King's Governor now rode emboldened. Many who had shouted more or less loudly for the rising star, now that it was so untimely set, made easy obeisance to the old sun. A great number who had wavered in the wind now declared that they had done no such thing, but had always stood steadfast for the ancient powers.

The old Governor, who might once have been magnanimous, was changed for the worse. He had been withstood; he would punish. He now gave full rein to his passionate temper, his bigotry for the throne, and his feeling of personal wrong. He began in Virginia to outlaw and arrest rebels, and to doom them to hasty trials and executions. There was no longer a united army to meet, but only groups and individuals striving for safety in flight or hiding. Hansford was early taken and hanged with two lieutenants of Bacon, Wilford and Farlow. Cheeseman died in prison. Drummond was taken in the swamps of the Chickahominy and carried before the Governor. Berkeley brought his hands together. "Mr. Drummond,

you are very welcome! I am more glad to see you
than any man in Virginia! Mr. Drummond you
shall be hanged in half an hour!" Not in half an
hour, but on the same day he was hanged, imper-
turbable Scot to the last. Lawrence, held by
many to have been more than Bacon the true
author of the attempt, either put an end to himself
or escaped northward, for he disappears from
history. "The last account of Mr. Lawrence was
from an uppermost plantation whence he and
four other desperadoes with horses, pistols, etc.,
marched away in a snow ankle-deep." They "were
thought to have cast themselves into a branch of
some river, rather than to be treated like Drummond." Thus came to early and untimely end
the ringleaders of Bacon's Rebellion. In all, by
the Governor's command, thirty-seven men suffered death by hanging.

There comes to us, down the centuries, the comment of that King for whom Berkeley was so
zealous, a man who fell behind his colonial Governor in singleness of interest but excelled him in
good nature. "That old fool," said the second
Charles, "has hanged more men in that naked
country than I have done for the murder of my
father!"

That letter which Berkeley had written some months before to his sovereign about the "waters of rebellion" was now seen to have borne fruit. In January, while the Governor was yet running down fugitives, confiscating lands, and hanging "traitors," a small fleet from England sailed in, bringing a regiment of "Red Coates," and with them three commissioners charged with the duty of bringing order out of confusion. These commissioners, bearing the King's proclamation of pardon to all upon submission, were kinder than the irascible and vindictive Governor of Virginia, and they succeeded at last in restraining his fury. They made their report to England, and after some months obtained a second royal proclamation censuring Berkeley's vengeful course, "so derogatory to our princely clemency," abrogating the Assembly's more violent acts, and extending full pardon to all concerned in the late "rebellion," saving only the arch-rebel Bacon — to whom perhaps it now made little difference if they pardoned him or not.

But with this piece of good nature, so characteristic of the second Charles, there came neither to the King in person not to England as a whole any appreciation of the true ills behind the Virginian

revolt, nor any attempt to relieve them. Along
with the King's first proclamation came instructions for the Governor. "You shall be no more
obliged to call an Assembly once every year, but
only once in two years. . . .   Also whensoever the
Assembly is called fourteen days shall be the time
prefixed for their sitting and no longer." And the
narrowed franchise that Bacon's Assembly had
widened is narrowed again. "You shall take care
that the members of the Assembly be elected only
by freeholders, as being more agreeable to the cus-
tom of England." Nor is the grant to Culpeper
and Arlington revoked. Nor, wider and deeper, are
the Navigation Laws in any wise bettered. No more
than before, no more indeed than a century later,
is there any conception that the child exists no
more for the parent than the parent for the child.

Sir William Berkeley's loyalty had in the end
overshot itself. His zeal fatigued the King, and in
1677 he was recalled to England. As Governor
of Virginia he had been long popular at first but
in his old age detested. He had great personal
courage, fidelity, and generosity for those things
that ran with the current of a deep and narrow soul. He passes from the New World stage,
a marked and tragic figure. Behind him his

vengeances displeased even loyalist Virginia, willing on the whole to let bygones be bygones among neighbors and kindred. It is said that, when his ship went down the river, bonfires were lighted and cannon and muskets fired for joy. And so beyond the eastward horizon fades the old reactionary.

Herbert Jeffreys and then Sir Henry Chicheley follow Berkeley as Governors of Virginia; they are succeeded by Lord Culpeper and he by Lord Howard of Effingham.   King Charles dies and James the Second rules in England. Culpeper and Effingham play the Governor merely for what they can get for themselves out of Virginia.[1]   The price of tobacco goes down, down.   The crops are too large; the old poor remedies of letting much acreage go unplanted, or destroying and burning where the measure of production is exceeded, and of petitions to the King, are all resorted to, but they procure little relief.   Virginia cannot be called prosperous. England hears that the people are still disaffected and unquiet — and England stolidly wonders why.

During the reign of the second Charles, Maryland had suffered from political unrest somewhat

[1] In 1684 the Crown purchased from Culpeper all his rights except in the Northern Neck.

less than Virginia. The autocracy of Maryland
was more benevolent and more temperate than
that of her southern neighbor. The name of Calvert is a better symbol of wisdom than the name
of Berkeley. Cecil Calvert, second Lord Baltimore,
dying in 1675, has a fair niche in the temple of
human enlightenment. His son Charles succeeded,
third Lord Baltimore and Lord Proprietary of
Maryland. Well-intentioned, this Calvert lacked
something of the ability of either his father or his
grandfather. Though he lived in Maryland while
his father had lived in England, his government
was not as wise as his father's had been.

But in Maryland, even before the death of Cecil
Calvert, inherent evils were beginning to form of
themselves a visible body. In Maryland, as in Virginia, there set in after the Restoration a period of
reaction, of callous rule in the interests of an oligarchy. In 1669 a "packed" Council and an "aristocratic" Assembly procured a restriction of the
franchise similar to that introduced into Virginia.
As in Virginia, an Assembly deemed of the right
political hue was kept in being by the device of
adjournment from year to year. In Maryland, as
in Virginia, public officials were guilty of corrup-
tion and graft. In 1676 there seems to have lacked

for revolt, in Maryland, only the immediate pro-
vocative of acute Indian troubles and such leaders
as Bacon, Lawrence, and Drummond. The new
Lord Baltimore being for the time in England, his
deputy writes him that never were any "more re-
plete with malignancy and frenzy than our people
were about August last, and they wanted but a
monstrous head to their monstrous body." Two
leaders indeed appeared, Davis and Pate by name,
but having neither the standing nor the strength
of the Virginia rebels, they were finally taken and
hanged. What supporters they had dispersed, and
the specter of armed insurrection passed away.

The third Lord Baltimore, like his father,
found difficulty in preserving the integrity of his
domain. His father had been involved in a long
wrangle over the alleged invasion of Maryland by
the Dutch. Since then, New Netherland had
passed into English hands. Now there occurred
another encroachment on the territory of Maryland. This time the invader was an Englishman
named William Penn. Just as the idea of a New
World freedom for Catholics had appealed to the
first Lord Baltimore, so now to William Penn, the
Quaker, came the thought of freedom there for
the Society of Friends. The second Charles owed

an old debt to Penn's father. He paid it in 1681 by giving to the son, whom he liked, a province in America. Little by little, in order to gain for Penn access to the sea, the terms of his grant were widened until it included, beside the huge Pennsylvanian region, the tract that is now Delaware, which was then claimed by Baltimore. Maryland protested against the grant to Penn, as Virginia had protested against the grant to Baltimore — and equally in vain. England was early set upon the road to many colonies in America, destined later to become many States. One by one they were carved out of the first great unity.

In 1685 the tolerant Charles the Second died. James the Second, a Catholic, ruled England for about three years, and then fled before the Revolution of 1688. William and Mary, sovereigns of a Protestant England, came to the throne. We have seen that the Proprietary of Maryland and his numerous kinsmen and personal adherents were Catholics. Approximately one in eight of other Marylanders were fellows in that faith. Another eighth of the people held with the Church of England. The rest, the mass of the folk, were dissenters from that Church. And now all the Protestant elements together — the Quakers ex-

cepted — solidified into political and religious opposition to the Proprietary's rule. Baltimore, still
in England, had immediately, upon the accession
of William and Mary, dispatched orders to the
Maryland Council to proclaim them King and
Queen. But his messenger died at sea, and there
was delay in sending another. In Maryland the
Council would not proclaim the new sovereigns
without instructions, and it was even rumored that
Catholic Maryland meant to withstand the new
order.

In effect the old days were over. The Protestants, Churchmen and Dissenters alike, proceeded
to organize under a new leader, one John Coode.
They formed "An Association in arms for the
defense of the Protestant religion, and for assert-
ing the right of King William and Queen Mary
to the Province of Maryland and all the English
Dominions." Now followed a confused time of accusations and counter-accusations, with assertions
that Maryland Catholics were conspiring with the
Indians to perpetrate a new St. Bartholomew
massacre of Protestants, and hot counter-asser-
tions that this is "a sleveless fear and imagination
fomented by the artifice of some ill-minded persons." In the end Coode assembled a force of

something less than a thousand men and marched against St. Mary's. The Council, which had gathered there, surrendered, and the Association for the Defense found itself in power. It proceeded to call a convention and to memorialize the King and Queen, who in the end approved its course. Maryland passed under the immediate government of the Crown. Lord Baltimore might still receive quit-rents and customs, but his governmental rights were absorbed into the monarchy. Sir Lionel Copley came out as Royal Governor, and a new order began in Maryland.

The heyday of Catholic freedom was past. England would have a Protestant America. Episcopalians were greatly in the minority, but their Church now became dominant over both Catholic and Dissenter, and where the freethinker raised his head he was smitten down. Catholic and Dissenter and all alike were taxed to keep stable the Established Church. The old tolerance, such as it was, was over. Maryland paced even with the rest of the world.

Presently the old capital of St. Mary's was abandoned. The government removed to the banks of the Severn, to Providence — soon, when Anne should be Queen, to be renamed Annapolis.

In vain the inhabitants of St. Mary's remonstrated. The center of political gravity in Maryland had shifted.

The third Lord Baltimore died in 1715. His son Benedict, fourth lord, turned from the Catholic Church and became a member of the Church of England. Dying presently, he left a young son, Charles, fifth Lord Baltimore, to be brought up in the fold of the Established Church. Reconciled now to the dominant creed, with a Maryland where Catholics were heavily penalized, Baltimore resumed the government under favor of the Crown. But it was a government with a difference. In Maryland, as everywhere, the people were beginning to hold the reins. Not again the old lord and the old underling! For years to come the lords would say that they governed, but strong life arose beneath, around, and above their governing.

Maryland had by 1715 within her bounds more than forty thousand white men and nearly ten thousand black men. She still planted and shipped tobacco, but presently found how well she might raise wheat, and that it, too, was valuable to send away in exchange for all kinds of manufactured things. Thus Maryland began to be a land of wheat still more than a land of tobacco.

For the rest, conditions of life in Maryland paralleled pretty closely those in Virginia. Maryland was almost wholly rural; her plantations and farms were reached with difficulty by roads hardly more than bridle-paths, or with ease by sailboat and rowboat along the innumerable waterways. Though here and there manors — large, easygoing, patriarchal places, with vague, feudal ways and customs — were to be found, the moderate sized plantation was the rule. Here stood, in sight usually of blue water, the planter's dwelling of brick or wood. Around it grew up the typical out-houses, household offices, and storerooms; farther away yet clustered the cabin quarters alike of slaves and indentured labor. Then stretched the fields of corn and wheat, the fields of tobacco. Here, at river or bay side, was the home wharf or landing. Here the tobacco was rolled in casks; here rattled the anchor of the ship that was to take it to England and bring in return a thousand and one manufactured articles. There were no fac-tories in Maryland or Virginia. Yet artisans were found among the plantation laborers — "carpen-ters, coopers, sawyers, blacksmiths, tanners, curri-ers, shoemakers, spinners, weavers, and knitters." Throughout the colonies, as in every new country, men and women, besides being agriculturists, produced homemade much that men, women, and children needed. But many other articles and all luxuries came in the ships from overseas, and the harvest of the fields paid the account.

CHAPTER XIV

THE CAROLINAS

THE first settlers on the banks of the James River, looking from beneath their hands southward over plain land and a haze of endless forests, called that unexplored country South Virginia. It stretched away to those rivers and bays, to that island of Roanoke, whence had fled Raleigh's settlers. Beyond that, said the James River men, was Florida. Time passed, and the region of South Virginia was occasionally spoken of as Carolina, though whether that name was drawn from Charles the First of England, or whether those old unfortunate Huguenots in Florida had used it with reference to Charles the Ninth of France, is not certainly known.

South Virginia lay huge, unknown, unsettled. The only exception was the country immediately below the southern banks of the lower James with the promontory that partially closed in Chesapeake

Bay. Virginia, growing fast, at last sent her children into this region. In 1653 the Assembly enacted: "Upon the petition of Roger Green, clarke, on the behalfe of himselfe and inhabitants of Nansemund river, It is ordered by this present Grand Assembly that tenn thousand acres of land be granted unto one hundred such persons who shall first seate on Moratuck or Roanoke river and the land lying upon the south side of Choan river and the branches thereof, Provided that such seaters settle advantageously for security and be sufficiently furnished with amunition and strength. . . ."

Green and his men, well furnished presumably with firelocks, bullets, and powder-horns, went into this hinterland. At intervals there followed other hardy folk. Quakers, subject to persecution in old Virginia, fled into these wilds. The name Carolina grew to mean backwoods, frontiersman's land. Here were forest and stream, Indian and bear and wolf, blue waters of sound and sea, long outward lying reefs and shoals and islets, fertile soil and a clime neither hot nor cold. Slowly the people increased in number. Families left settled Virginia for the wilderness; men without families came there for reasons good and bad. Their cabins, their tiny

hamlets were far apart; they practised a hazardous
agriculture; they hunted, fished, and traded with
the Indians.   The isolation of these settlers bred
or increased their personal independence, while
it robbed them of that smoothness to be gained
where the social particles rub together. This part
of South Virginia was soon to be called North
Carolina.

Far down the coast was Cape Fear. In the year
of the Restoration a handful of New England men
came here in a ship and made a settlement which,
not prospering, was ere long abandoned.   But
New Englanders traded still in South Virginia
as along other coasts.   Seafarers, they entered
at this inlet and at that, crossed the wide blue
sounds, and, anchoring in mouths of rivers, purchased from the settlers their forest commodities.
Then over they ran to the West Indies, and got
in exchange sugar and rum and molasses, with
which again they traded for tobacco in Carolina,
in Virginia, and in Maryland.   These ships went
often to New Providence in the Bahamas and to
Barbados.   There began, through trade and other
circumstances, a special connection between the
long coast line and these islands that were peopled
by the English.

The restored Kingdom of England had many adherents to reward. Land in America, islands and main, formed the obvious Fortunatus's purse. As the second Charles had divided Virginia for the benefit of Arlington and Culpeper, so now, in 1663, to "our right trusty and right well-beloved cousins and counsellors, Edward, Earl of Clarendon, our High Chancellor of England, and George, Duke of Albemarle, Master of our Horse and Captain-General of all our Forces, our right trusty and well-beloved William, Lord Craven, John, Lord Berkeley, our right trusty and well-beloved counsellor, Anthony, Lord Ashley, Chancellor of our Exchequer, Sir George Carteret, Knight and Baronet, Vice-Chamberlain of our Household, and our trusty and well-beloved Sir William Berkeley, Knight, and Sir John Colleton, Knight and Baronet," he gave South Virginia, henceforth called the Carolinas, a region occupying five degrees of latitude, and stretching indefinitely from the seacoast toward the setting sun.

This huge territory became, like Maryland, a province or palatinate. In Maryland was one Proprietary; in Carolina there were eight, though for distinction the senior of the eight was called the Palatine. As in Maryland, the Proprietaries had princely rights. They owed allegiance to England, and a small quit-rent went to the King. They were supposed to govern, in the main, by English law and to uphold the religion of England. They were to make laws at their discretion, with "the advice, assent, and approbation of the freemen, or of their deputies, who were to be assembled from time to time as seemed best."

John Locke, who wrote the *Essay Concerning Human Understanding*, wrote also, with Ashley at his side, *The Fundamental Constitutions of Carolina, in number a Hundred and Twenty, agreed upon by the Palatine and Lords Proprietors, to remain the sacred and unalterable form and Rule of government of Carolina forever.*

"Forever" is a long word with ofttimes a short history. The Lords Proprietors have left their names upon the maps of North and South Carolina. There are Albemarle Sound and the Ashley and Cooper rivers, Clarendon, Hyde, Carteret, Craven, and Colleton Counties. But their Fundamental Constitutions, "in number a hundred and twenty," written by Locke in 1669, are almost all as dead as the leaves of the Carolina forest falling in the autumn of that year.

The grant included that territory settled by

Roger Green and his men. Among the Proprietors sat Sir William Berkeley, Governor of Virginia, the only lord of Carolina actually upon American ground. Following instructions from his seven fellows Berkeley now declared this region separated from Virginia and attached to Carolina. He christened it Albemarle. Strangely enough, he sent as Governor that Scotchman, William Drummond, whom some years later he would hang. Drummond should have a Council of six and an Assembly of freemen that might inaugurate legislation having to do with local matters but must submit its acts to the Proprietaries for veto or approval. This was the settlement in Carolina of Albemarle, back country to Virginia, gatherer thence of many that were hardy and sound, many that were unfortunate, and many that were shiftless and untamed. An uncouth nurse of a turbulent democracy was Albemarle.

Cape Fear, far down the deeply frayed coast, seemed a proper place to which to send a colony. The intrusive Massachusetts men were gone. But "gentlemen and merchants" of Barbados were interested. It is a far cry from Barbados to the Carolina shore, but so is it a far cry from England. Many royalists had fled to Barbados during the old troubles, so that its English population was considerable. A number may have welcomed the chance to leave their small island for the immense continent; and an English trading port as far south as Cape Fear must have had a general appeal. So, in 1665, came Englishmen from Barbados and made, up the Cape Fear River, a settlement which they named Clarendon, with John Yeamans of Barbados as Governor. But the colony did not prosper. There arose the typical colonial troubles — sickness, dissensions, improvidence, quarrels with the aborigines. Nor was the site the best obtainable. The settlers finally abandoned the place and scattered to various points along the northern coast.

In 1669 the Lords Proprietaries sent out from England three ships, the *Carolina*, the *Port Royal*, and the *Albemarle*, with about a hundred colonists aboard. Taking the old sea road, they came at last to Barbados, and here the *Albemarle*, seized by a storm, was wrecked. The two other ships, with a Barbados sloop, sailed on and were approaching the Bahamas when another hurricane destroyed the *Port Royal*. The *Carolina*, however, pushed on with the sloop, reached Bermuda, and rested there: then, together with a small ship purchased in these islands, she turned west by south and came in March of 1670 to the good harbor of Port Royal, South Carolina.

Southward from the harbor where the ships rode, stretched old Florida, held by the Spaniards. There was the Spanish town, St. Augustine. Thence Spanish ships might put forth and descend upon the English newcomers. The colonists after debate concluded to set some further space between them and lands of Spain. The ships put again to sea, beat northward a few leagues, and at last entered a harbor into which emptied two rivers, presently to be called the Ashley and the Cooper. Up the Ashley they went a little way, anchored, and the colonists going ashore began to build upon the west bank of the river a town which for the King they named Charles Town. Ten years later this place was abandoned in favor of the more convenient point of land between the two rivers. Here then was builded the second and more enduring Charles Town — Charleston, as we call it now, in South Carolina.

Colonists came fast to this Carolina lying south. Barbados sent many; England, Scotland, and Ireland contributed a share; there came Huguenots from France, and a certain number of Germans.

In ten years after the first settling the population numbered twelve hundred, and this presently doubled and went on to increase. The early times were taken up with the wrestle with the forest, with the Indians, with Spanish alarms, with incompetent governors, with the Lords Proprietaries' Fundamental Constitutions, and with the restrictions which English Navigation Laws imposed upon English colonies. What grains and vegetables and tobacco they could grow, what cattle and swine they could breed and export, preoccupied the minds of these pioneer farmers. There were struggling for growth a rough agriculture and a hampered trade with Barbados, Virginia, and New England — trade likewise with the buccaneers who swarmed in the West Indian waters.

Five hundred good reasons allowed, and had long allowed, freebootery to flourish in American seas. Gross governmental faults, Navigation Acts, and a hundred petty and great oppressions, general poverty, adventurousness, lawlessness, and sympathy of mishandled folk with lawlessness, all combined to keep Brother of the Coast, Buccaneer, and Filibuster alive, and their ships upon all seas. Many were no worse than smugglers; others were robbers with violence; and a few had a dash of the fiend. All nations had sons in the business. England to the south in America had just the ragged coast line, with its off-lying islands and islets, liked by all this gentry, whether smuggler or pirate outright. Through much of the seventeenth century the settlers on these shores never violently disapproved of the pirate. He was often a "good fellow." He brought in needed articles without dues, and had Spanish gold in his pouch. He was shrugged over and traded with.

He came ashore to Charles Town, and they traded with him there. At one time Charles Town got the name of "Rogue's Harbor." But that was not forever, nor indeed, as years are counted, for long. Better and better emigrants arrived, to add to the good already there. The better type prevailed, and gave its tone to the place. There set in, on the Ashley and Cooper rivers, a fair urban life that yet persists.

South Carolina was trying tobacco and wheat. But in the last years of the seventeenth century a ship touching at Charleston left there a bag of Madagascar rice. Planted, it gave increase that was planted again. Suddenly it was found that this was the crop for low-lying Carolina. Rice became her staple, as was tobacco of Virginia.

For the rice-fields South Carolina soon wanted African slaves, and they were consequently brought in numbers, in English ships. There began, in this part of the world, even more than in Virginia, the system of large plantations and the accompanying aristocratic structure of society. But in Virginia the planter families lived broadcast over the land, each upon its own plantation. In South Carolina, to escape heat and sickness, the planters of rice and indigo gave over to employees the care of their great holdings and lived themselves in pleasant Charleston. These plantations, with their great gangs of slaves under overseers, differed at many points from the more kindly, semi-patriarchal life of the Virginian plantation. To South Carolina came also the indentured white laborer, but the black was imported in increasing numbers.

From the first in the Carolinas there had been promised fair freedom for the unorthodox. The charters provided, says an early Governor, "an overplus power to grant liberty of conscience, although at home was a hot persecuting time." Huguenots, Independents, Quakers, dissenters of many kinds, found on the whole refuge and harbor. In every colony soon began the struggle by the dominant color and caste toward political liberty.

King, Company, Lords Proprietaries, might strive to rule from over the seas. But the new land fast bred a practical rough freedom. The English settlers came out from a land where political change was in the air. The stream was set toward the crumbling of feudalism, the rise of democracy. In the New World, circumstances favoring, the stream became a tidal river. Governors, councils, assemblies, might use a misleading phraseology of a quaint servility toward the constituted powers in England. Tory parties might at times seem to color the land their own hue. But there always ran, though often roughly and with turbulence, a set of the stream against autocracy.

In Carolina, South and North, by the Ashley and Cooper rivers, and in that region called Albemarle, just back of Virginia, there arose and went on, through the remainder of the seventeenth century and in the eighteenth, struggles with the Lords Proprietaries and the Governors that these named, and behind this a more covert struggle with the Crown. The details differed, but the issues involved were much the same in North and South Carolina. The struggle lasted for the threescore and odd years of the proprietary government and renewed itself upon occasion after 1729 when the Carolinas became royal colonies. Later, it was swept, a strong affluent, into the great general stream of colonial revolt, culminating in the Revolution.

Into North Carolina, beside the border population entering through Virginia and containing much of a backwoods and derelict nature, came many Huguenots, the best of folk, and industrious Swiss, and Germans from the Rhine. Then the Scotch began to come in numbers, and families of Scotch descent from the north of Ireland. The tone of society consequently changed from that of the early days. The ruffian and the shiftless sank to the bottom. There grew up in North Carolina a people, agricultural but without great plantations, hard-working and freedom-loving.

South Carolina, on the other hand, had great plantations, a town society, suave and polished, a learned clergy, an aristocratic cast to life. For long, both North and South clung to the sea-line and to the lower stretches of rivers where the ships could come in. Only by degrees did English colonial life push back into the forests away from the sea, to the hills, and finally across the mountains.

CHAPTER XV

ALEXANDER SPOTSWOOD

In the spring of 1689, Virginians flocked to Jamestown to hear William and Mary proclaimed Lord
and Lady of Virginia. The next year there entered, as Lieutenant-Governor, Francis Nicholson,
an odd character in whom an immediate violence
of temper went with a statesmanlike conception
of things to be. Two years he governed here, then
was transferred to Maryland, and then in seven
years came back to the James. He had not been
liked there, but while he was gone Virginia had
endured in his stead Sir Edmund Andros. That
had been swapping the witch for the devil. Virginia in 1698 seems to have welcomed the returning
Nicholson.

Jamestown had been hastily rebuilt, after Bacon's burning, and then by accident burned again.
The word malaria was not in use, but all knew
that there had always been sickness on that low

spit running out from the marshes. The place
might well seem haunted, so many had suffered
there and died there. Poetical imagination might
have evoked a piece of sad pageantry—starving
times, massacres, quarrels, executions, cruel and
unusual punishments, gliding Indians. A practical question, however, faced the inhabitants,
and all were willing to make elsewhere a new
capital city.

Seven miles back from the James, about half-
way over to the blue York, stood that cluster of
houses called Middle Plantation, where Bacon's
men had taken his Oath. There was planned and
builded Williamsburg, which was to be for nearly
a hundred years the capital of Virginia. It was
named for King William, and there was in the
minds of some loyal colonists the notion, eventually abandoned, of running the streets in the
lines of a huge W and M. The long main street
was called Duke of Gloucester Street, for the short-
lived son of that Anne who was soon to become
Queen. At one end of this thoroughfare stood a
fair brick capitol. At the other end nearly a mile
away rose the brick William and Mary College.
Its story is worth the telling.

The formal acquisition of knowledge had long

been a problem in Virginia. Adult colonists came with their education, much or little, gained already in the mother country. In most cases, doubtless, it was little, but in many cases it was much. Books were brought in with other household furnishing. When there began to be native-born Virginians, these children received from parents and kindred some manner of training. Ministers were supposed to catechise and teach. Well-to-do and educated parents brought over tutors. Promising sons were sent to England to school and university. But the lack of means to knowledge for the mass of the colony began to be painfully apparent.

In the time of Charles the First one Benjamin Symms had left his means for the founding of a free school in Elizabeth County, and his action had been solemnly approved by the Assembly. By degrees there appeared other similar free schools, though they were never many nor adequate. But the first Assembly after the Restoration had made provision for a college. Land was to have been purchased and the building completed as speedily as might be. The intent had been good, but nothing more had been done.

There was in Virginia, sent as Commissioner of

the Established Church, a Scotch ecclesiastic, Dr. James Blair. In virtue of his office he had a seat in the Council, and his integrity and force soon made him a leader in the colony. A college in Virginia became Blair's dream. He was supported by Virginia planters with sons to educate — daughters' education being purely a domestic affair. Before long Blair had raised in promised subscriptions what was for the time a large sum. With this for a nucleus he sailed to England and there collected more. Tillotson, Archbishop of Canterbury, and Stillingfleet, Bishop of Worcester, helped him much. The King and Queen inclined a favorable ear, and, though he met with opposition in certain quarters, Blair at last obtained his charter. There was to be built in Virginia and to be sustained by taxation a great school, "a seminary of ministers of the gospel where youths may be piously educated in good letters and manners; a certain place of universal study, or perpetual college of divinity, philosophy, languages and other good arts and sciences." Blair sailed back to Virginia with the charter of the college, some money, a plan for the main building drawn by Christopher Wren, and for himself the office of President.

The Assembly, for the benefit of the college,

taxed raw and tanned hides, dressed buckskin, skins of doe and elk, muskrat and raccoon. The construction of the new seat of learning was begun at Williamsburg. When it was completed and opened to students, it was named William and Mary. Its name and record shine fair in old Virginia. Colonial worthies in goodly number were educated at William and Mary, as were later revolutionary soldiers and statesmen, and men of name and fame in the United States. Three American Presidents — Jefferson, Monroe, and Tyler — were trained there, as well as Marshall, the Chief Justice, four signers of the Declaration of Independence, and many another man of mark.

The seventeenth century is about to pass. France and England are at war. The colonial air vibrates with the struggle. There is to be a brief lull after 1697, but the conflict will soon be resumed. The more northerly colonies, the nearer to New France, feel the stronger pulsation, but Virginia, too, is shaken. England and France alike play for the support of the red man. All the western side of America lies open to incursion from that pressed-back Indian sea of unknown extent and volume. Up and down, the people, who have had no part in making that European war, are sensitive to the menace of its dangers. In Virginia they build blockhouses and they keep rangers on guard far up the great rivers.

All the world is changing, and the changes are fraught with significance for America. Feudalism has passed; scholasticism has gone; politics, commerce, philosophy, religion, science, invention, music, art, and literature are rapidly altering. In England William and Mary pass away. Queen Anne begins her reign of twelve years. Then, in 1714, enters the House of Hanover with George the First. It is the day of Newton and Locke and Berkeley, of Hume, of Swift, Addison, Steele, Pope, Prior, and Defoe. The great romantic sixteenth century, Elizabeth's spacious time, is gone. The deep and narrow, the intense, religious, individualistic seventeenth century is gone. The eighteenth century, immediate parent of the nineteenth, grandparent of the twentieth, occupies the stage.

In the year 1704, just over a decade since Dr. Blair had obtained the charter for his College, the erratic and able Governor of Virginia, Francis Nicholson, was recalled. For all that he was a wild talker, he had on the whole done well for Virginia.

He was, as far as is known, the first person actually to propose a federation or union of all those English-speaking political divisions, royal provinces, dominions, palatinates, or what not, that had been hewed away from the vast original Virginia. He did what he could to forward the movement for education and the fortunes of the William and Mary College. But he is quoted as having on one occasion informed the body of the people that "the gentlemen imposed upon them." Again, he is said to have remarked of the servant population that they had all been kidnapped and had a lawful action against their masters. "Sir," he stated to President Blair, who would have given him advice from the Bishop of London, "Sir, I know how to govern Virginia and Maryland better than all the bishops in England! If I had not hampered them in Maryland and kept them under, I should never have been able to govern them!" To which Blair had to say, "Sir, if I know anything of Virginia, they are a good-natured, tractable people as any in the world, and you may do anything with them by way of civility, but you will never be able to manage them in that way you speak of, by hampering and keeping them under!"[1]

[1] *William and Mary College Quarterly*, vol. I, p. 66.

About this time arrived Claude de Richebourg with a number of Huguenots who settled above the Falls. First and last, Virginia received many of this good French strain. The Old Dominion had now a population of over eighty thousand persons — whites, Indians in no great number, and negroes. The red men are mere scattered dwellers in the land east of the mountains. There are Indian villages, but they are far apart. Save upon the frontier fringe, the Indian attacks no more. But the African is here to stay.

The Negroes live in small Cottages called Quarters . . . under the direction of an Overseer or Bailiff; who takes care that they tend such Land as the Owner allots and orders, upon which they raise Hogs and Cattle and plant Indian Corn, and Tobacco for the Use of their Master. . . . The Negroes are very numerous, some Gentlemen having Hundreds of them of all Sorts, to whom they bring great Profitt; for the Sake of which they are obliged to keep them well, and not over-work, starve or famish them, besides other Inducements to favour them; which is done in a great Degree, to such especially that are laborious, careful and honest; tho' indeed some Masters, careless of their own Interest or Reputation, are too cruel and negligent. The Negroes are not only encreased by fresh supplies from Africa and the West India Islands, but also are very prolific araong themselves; and they that are born here talk good English and affect our Language, Habits and

Customs. . . . Their work (or Chimerical hard Slav‹ery) is not very laborious; their greatest Hardship consisting in that they and their Posterity are not at their own Liberty or Disposal, but are the Property of their Owners; and when they are free they know not how to provide so well for themselves generally; neither did they live so plentifully nor (many of them) so easily in their own Country where they are made Slaves to one another, or taken Captive by their Ennemies.[1]

The white Virginians lived both after the fashion of England and after fashions made by their New World environment. They are said to have been in general a handsome folk, tall, well-formed, and with a ready and courteous manner. They were great lovers of riding, and of all country life, and few folk in the world might overpass them in hospitality. They were genial, they liked a good laugh, and they danced to good music. They had by nature an excellent understanding. Yet, thinks at least the Reverend Hugh Jones, they "are generally diverted by Business or Inclination from profound Study, and prying into the Depth of Things. . . . They are more inclinable to read

[1] It is an English clergyman, the Reverend Hugh Jones, who is writing (*The Present State of Virginia*) in the year 1724. He writes and never sees that, though every amelioration be true, yet there is here old Inequity.

Men by Business and Conversation, than to dive into Books . . . they are apt to learn, yet they are fond of and will follow their own Ways, Humours and Notions, being not easily brought to new Projects and Schemes."

It was as Governor of these people that, in succession to Nicholson, Edward Nott came to Virginia, the deputy of my Lord Orkney. Nott died soon afterward, and in 1710 Orkney sent to Virginia in his stead Alexander Spotswood. This man stands in Virginia history a manly, honorable, popular figure. Of Scotch parentage, born in Morocco, soldier under Marlborough, wounded at Blenheim, he was yet in his thirties when he sailed across the Atlantic to the river James. Virginia liked him, and he liked Virginia. A man of energy and vision, he first made himself at home with all, and then after his own impulses and upon his own lines went about to develop and to better the colony. He had his projects and his hobbies, mostly useful, and many sounding with a strong modern tone. Now and again he quarreled with the Assembly, and he made it many a cutting speech. But it, too, and all Virginia and the world were growing modern. Issues were disengaging themselves and were becoming distinct. In these early years of the eighteenth century, Whig and Tory in England drew sharply over against each other. In Virginia, too, as in Maryland, the Carolinas, and all the rest of England-in-America, parties were emerging. The Virginian *flair* for political life was thus early in evidence. To the careless eye the colony might seem overwhelmingly for King and Church. "If New England be called a Receptacle of Dissenters, and an Amsterdam of Religion, Pennsylvania the Nursery of Quakers, Maryland the Retirement of Roman Catholicks, North Carolina the Refuge of Runaways and South Carolina the Delight of Buccaneers and Pyrates, Virginia may be justly esteemed the happy Retreat of true Britons and true Churchmen for the most Part." This "for the most part" paints the situation, for there existed an opposition, a minority, which might grow to balance, and overbalance. In the meantime the House of Burgesses at Williamsburg provided a School for Discussion.

At the time when Parson Jones with his shrewd eyes was observing society in the Old Dominion, Williamsburg was still a small village, even though it was the capital. Towns indeed, in any true sense. were nowhere to be found in Virginia. Ye*

Williamsburg had a certain distinction. Within it there arose, beneath and between old forest trees, the college, an admirable church — Bruton Church — the capitol, the Governor's house or "palace," and many very tolerable dwelling-houses of frame and brick. There were also taverns, a market-place, a bowling-green, an arsenal, and presently a playhouse. The capitol at Williamsburg was a commodious one, able to house most of the machinery of state. Here were the Council Chamber, "where the Governor and Council sit in very great state, in imitation of the King and Council, or the Lord Chancellor and House of Lords," and the great room of the House of Burgesses, "not unlike the House of Commons." Here, at the capitol met the General Courts in April and October, the Governor and Council acting as judges. There were also Oyer and Terminer and Admiralty Courts. There were offices and committee rooms, and on the cupola a great clock, and near the capitol was "a strong, sweet Prison for Criminals; and on the other side of an open Court another for Debtors . . . but such Prisoners are very rare, the Creditors being generally very merciful. . . . At the Capitol, at publick Times, may be seen a great Number of handsome, well-dressed, compleat Gentlemen. And at the Governor's House upon Birth-Nights, and at Balls and Assemblies, I have seen as fine an Appearance, as good Diversion, and as splendid Entertainments, in Governor Spotswood's Time, as I have seen anywhere else."

It is a far cry from the *Susan Constant*, the *Goodspeed*, and the *Discovery*, from those first booths at Jamestown, from the Starving Time, from Christopher Newport and Edward-Maria Wingfield and Captain John Smith to these days of Governor Spotswood. And yet, considering the changes still to come, a century seems but a little time and the far cry not so very far.

Though the Virginians were in the mass country folk, yet villages or hamlets arose, clusters of houses pressing about the Court House of each county. There were now in the colony over a score of settled counties. The westernmost of these, the frontier counties, were so huge that they ran at least to the mountains, and, for all one knew to the contrary, presumably beyond. But "beyond" was a mysterious word of unknown content, for no Virginian of that day had gone beyond. All the way from Canada into South Carolina and the Florida of that time stretched the mighty sys tem of the Appalachians, fifteen hundred miles in length and three hundred in breadth. Here was a barrier long and thick, with ridge after ridge of lifted and forested earth, with knife-blade vales between, and only here and there a break away and an encompassed treasure of broad and fertile valley. The Appalachians made a true Chinese Wall, shutting all England-in-America, in those early days, out from the vast inland plateau of the continent, keeping upon the seaboard all England-in-America, from the north to the south. To Virginia these were the mysterious mountains just beyond which, at first, were held to be the South Sea and Cathay. Now, men's knowledge being larger by a hundred years, it was known that the South Sea could not be so near. The French from Canada, going by way of the St. Lawrence and the Great Lakes, had penetrated very far beyond and had found not the South Sea but a mighty river flowing into the Gulf of Mexico. What was the real nature of this world which had been found to lie over the mountains? More and more Virginians were inclined to find out, foreseeing that they would need room for their growing population. Continuously came in folk from the Old Country, and continuously Virginians were

born.   Maryland dwelt to the north, Carolina to
the south.   Virginia, seeking space, must begin to
grow westward.

There were settlements from the sea to the
Falls of the James, and upon the York, the Rappahannock, and the Potomac.   Beyond these, in the
wilderness, might be found a few lonely cabins, a
scattered handful of pioneer folk, small blockhouses, and small companies of rangers charged
with protecting all from Indian foray.   All this
country was rolling and hilly, but beyond it stood
the mountains, a wall of enchantment, against the
west.

Alexander Spotswood, hardy Scot, endowed with
a good temperamental blend of the imaginative
and the active, was just the man, the time being
ripe, to encounter and surmount that wall.   Fortunately, too, the Virginians were horsemen, man
and horse one piece almost, New World centaurs.
They would follow the bridle-tracks that pierced
to the hilly country, and beyond that they might
yet make way through the primeval forest.   They
would encounter dangers, but hardly the old perils
of seacoast and foothills.   Different, indeed, is this
adventure of the Governor of Virginia and his
chosen band from the old push afoot into frowning

hostile woods by the men of a hundred and odd years before!

Spotswood rode westward with a company drawn largely from the colonial gentry, men young in body or in spirit, gay and adventurous. The whole expedition was conceived and executed in a key both humorous and knightly. These "Knights"[1] set face toward the mountains in August, 1716. They had guides who knew the up-country, a certain number of rangers used to Indian ways, and servants with food and much wine in their charge. So out of settled Virginia they rode, and up the long, gradual lift of earth above sea-level into a mountainous wilderness, where before them the Aryan had not come. By day they traveled, and bivouacked at night.

Higher and more rugged grew the mountains. Some trick of the light made them show blue, so that they presently came to be called the Blue

[1] On the sandy roads of settled Virginia horses went unshod, but for the stony hills and the ultimate cliffs they must have iron shoes. After the adventure and when the party had returned to civilization, the Governor, bethinking himself that there should be some token and memento of the exploit, had made in London a number of small golden horseshoes, set as pins to be worn in the lace cravats of the period. Each adventurer to the mountains received one, and the band has kept, in Virginian lore, the title of the Knights of the Golden Horseshoe.

Ridge, in contradistinction to the westward lying, gray Alleghanies. They were like very long ocean combers, with at intervals an abrupt break, a gap, cliff-guarded, boulder-strewn, with a narrow rushing stream making way between hemlocks and pines, sycamore, ash and beech, walnut and linden.

Towards these blue mountains Spotswood and his knights rode day after day and came at last to the foot of the steep slope. The long ridges were high, but not so high but that horse and man might make shift to scramble to the crest. Up they climbed and from the heights they looked across and down into the Valley of Virginia, twenty miles wide, a hundred and twenty long — a fertile garden spot. Across the shimmering distances they saw the gray Alleghanies, fresh barrier to a fresh west. Below them ran a clear river, afterwards to be called the Shenandoah. They gazed — they predicted colonists, future plantations, future towns, for that great valley, large indeed as are some Old World kingdoms. They drank the health of England's King, and named two outstanding peaks Mount George and Mount Alexander; then, because their senses were ravished by the Eden before them, they dubbed the river Euphrates. They plunged and scrambled down the mountain side to the Euphrates, drank of it, bathed in it, rested, ate, and drank again. The deep green woods were around them; above them they could see the hawk, the eagle, and the buzzard, and at their feet the bright fish of the river.

At last they reclimbed the Blue Ridge, descended its eastern face, and, leaving the great wave of it behind them, rode homeward to Williamsburg in triumph.

We are thus, with Spotswood and his band, on the threshold of expanding American vistas. This Valley of Virginia, first a distant Beulah land for the eye of the imagination only, presently became a land of pioneer cabins, far apart—very far apart — then a settled land, of farms, hamlets, and market towns. Nor did the folk come only from that elder Virginia of tidal waters and much tobacco, of "compleat gentlemen" at the capital, and of many slaves in the fields. But downward from the Potomac, they came south into this valley, from Pennsylvania and Maryland, many of them Ulster Scots who had sailed to the western world. In America they are called the Scotch-Irish, and in the main they brought stout hearts, long arms, and level heads. With these they brought in as luggage the dogmas of Calvin.   They permeated the Valley of Virginia; many moved on south into Carolina; finally, in large part, they made Kentucky and Tennessee.   Germans, too, came into the valley—down from Pennsylvania-- quiet, thrifty folk, driven thus far westward from a war-ravished Rhine.

Shrewd practicality trod hard upon the heels of romantic fancy in the mind of Spotswood.   His Order of the Knights of the Horseshoe had a fleeting existence, but the Vision of the West lived on.   Frontier folk in growing numbers were encouraged to make their way from tidewater to the foot of the Blue Ridge.   Spotsylvania and King George were names given to new counties in the Piedmont in honor of the Governor and the sovereign.   German craftsmen, who had been sent over by Queen Anne—vine-dressers and ironworkers— were settled on Spotswood's own estate above the falls of the Rapidan.   The little town of Germanna sprang up, famous for its smelting furnaces.

To his country seat in Spotsylvania, Alexander Spotswood retired when he laid down the office of Governor in 1722.   But his talents were too valuable to be allowed to rust in inactivity.   He was appointed deputy Postmaster-General for the

English colonies, and in the course of his administration made one Benjamin Franklin Postmaster
for Philadelphia.   He was on the point of sailing
with Admiral Vernon on the expedition against
Cartagena in 1740, when he was suddenly stricken
and died.   He was buried at Temple Farm by
Yorktown.   On the expedition to Cartagena went
one Lawrence Washington, who named his country-
seat after the Admiral and whose brother George
many years later was to receive the surrender of
Cornwallis and his army hard by the resting-place
of Alexander Spotswood.   Colonial Virginia lies
behind us.   The era of revolution and statehood
beckons us on.

CHAPTER XVI

GEORGIA

BELOW Charleston in South Carolina, below Cape Fear, below Port Royal, a great river called the Savannah poured into the sea. Below the Savannah, past the Ogeechee, sailing south between the sandy islands and the main, ships came to the mouth of the river Altamaha. Thus far was Carolina. But below Altamaha the coast and the country inland became debatable, probably Florida and Spanish, liable at any rate to be claimed as such, and certainly open to attack from Spanish St. Augustine.

Here lay a stretch of seacoast and country within hailing distance of semi-tropical lands. It was low and sandy, with innumerable slow-flowing water-courses, creeks, and inlets from the sea. The back country, running up to hills and even mountains stuffed with ores, was not known — though indeed Spanish adventurers had wandered there and mined for gold. But the lowlands were warm and dense with trees and wild life. The Huguenot Ribault, making report of this region years and years before, called it "a fayre coast stretching of a great length, covered with an infinite number of high and fayre trees," and he described the land as the "fairest, fruitfullest, and pleasantest of all the world, abounding in hony, venison, wilde fowle, forests, woods of all sorts, Palm-trees, Cypresse and Cedars, Bayes ye highest and greatest; with also the fayrest vines in all the world. . . . And the sight of the faire medows is a pleasure not able to be expressed with tongue; full of Hernes, Curlues, Bitters, Mallards, Egrepths, Woodcocks, and all other kind of small birds; with Harts, Hindes, Buckes, wilde Swine, and all other kindes of wilde beastes, as we perceived well, both by their footing there and . . . their crie and roaring in the night."[1] This is the country of the live-oak and the magnolia, the gray, swinging moss and the yellow jessamine, the chameleon and the mocking-bird.

The Savannah and Altamaha rivers and the wide and deep lands between fell in that grant of Charles II's to the eight Lords Proprietors of Caro-

[1] Winsor's *Narrative and Critical History of America*, vol. v, p. 357.

lina — Albemarle, Clarendon, and the rest. But this region remained as yet unpeopled save by copper-hued folk. True, after the "American Treaty" of 1670 between England and Spain, the English built a small fort upon Cumberland Island, south of the Altamaha, and presently another — Fort George — to the northwest of the first, at the confluence of the rivers Oconee and Ocmulgee. There were, however, no true colonists between the Savannah and the Altamaha.

In the year 1717 — the year after Spotswood's Expedition — the Carolina Proprietaries granted to one Sir Robert Mountgomery all the land between the rivers Savannah and Altamaha, "with proper jurisdictions, privileges, prerogatives, and franchises." The arrangement was feudal enough. The new province was to be called the Margravate of Azilia. Mountgomery, as Margrave, was to render to the Lords of Carolina an annual quit-rent and one-fourth part of all gold and silver found in Azilia. He must govern in accordance with the laws of England, must uphold the established religion of England, and provide by taxation for the maintenance of the clergy. In three years' time the new Margrave must colonize his Margravate, and if he failed to do so, all his rights would disappear and Azilia would again dissolve into Carolina.

This was what happened. For whatever reason, Mountgomery could not obtain his colonists. Azilia remained a paper land. The years went by. The country, unsettled yet, lapsed into the Carolina from which so tentatively it had been parted. Over its spaces the Indian still roved, the tall forests still lifted their green crowns, and no axe was heard nor any English voice.

In the decade that followed, the Lords Proprietors of Carolina ceased to be Lords Proprietors. Their government had been, save at exceptional moments, confused, oppressive, now absent-minded, and now mistaken and arbitrary. They had meant very well, but their knowledge was not exact, and now virtual revolution in South Carolina assisted their demise. After lengthy negotiations, at last, in 1729, all except Lord Granville surrendered to the Crown, for a considerable sum, their rights and interests. Carolina, South and North, thereupon became royal colonies.

In England there dwelled a man named James Edward Oglethorpe, son of Sir Theophilus Oglethorpe of Godalming in Surrey. Though entered at Oxford, he soon left his books for the army and was present at the siege and taking of Belgrade in 1717. Peace descending, the young man returned to England, and on the death of his elder brother came into the estate, and was presently made Member of Parliament for Haslemere in Surrey.

His character was a firm and generous one; his bent, markedly humane. "Strong benevolence of soul," Pope says he had. His century, too, was becoming humane, was inquiring into ancient wrongs. There arose, among other things, a belated notion of prison reform. The English Parliament undertook an investigation, and Oglethorpe was of those named to examine conditions and to make a report. He came into contact with the incarcerated — not alone with the law-breaker, hardened or yet to be hardened, but with the wrongfully imprisoned and with the debtor. The misery of the debtor seems to have struck with insistent hand upon his heart's door. The parliamentary inquiry was doubtless productive of some good, albeit evidently not of great good. But though the inquiry was over, Oglethorpe's concern was not over. It brooded, and, in the inner clear light where ideas grow, eventually brought forth results.

Numbers of debtors lay in crowded and noisome English prisons, there often from no true fault at all, at times even because of a virtuous action, oftenest from mere misfortune. If they might but start again, in a new land, free from entanglements! Others, too, were in prison, whose crimes were negligible, mere mistaken moves with no evil will behind them — or, if not so negligible, then happening often through that misery and ignorance for which the whole world was at fault. There was also the broad and well-filled prison of poverty, and many of the prisoners there needed only a better start. James Edward Oglethorpe conceived another settlement in America, and for colonists he would have all these down-trodden and oppressed. He would gather, if he might, only those who when helped would help themselves — who when given opportunity would rise out of old slough and briar. He was personally open to the appeal of still another class of unfortunate men. He had seen upon the Continent the distress of the poor and humble Protestants in Catholic countries. Folk of this kind — from France, from Germany — had been going in a thin stream for years to the New World. But by his plan more might be enabled to escape petty tyranny or persecution.

He had influence, and his scheme appealed to the humane thought of his day — appealed, too, to the political thought. In America there was that debatable and unoccupied land south of Charles Town in South Carolina. It would be very good to settle it, and none had taken up the idea with seriousness since Azilia had failed. Such a colony as was now contemplated would dispose of Spanish claims, serve as a buffer colony between Florida and South Carolina, and establish another place of trade. The upshot was that the Crown granted to Oglethorpe and twenty associates the unsettled land between the Savannah and the Altamaha, with a westward depth that was left quite indefinite. This territory, which was now severed from Carolina, was named Georgia after his Majesty King George II, and Oglethorpe and a number of prominent men became the trustees of the new colony. They were to act as such for twenty-one years, at the end of which time Georgia should pass under the direct government of the Crown. Parliament gave to the starting of things ten thousand pounds, and wealthy philanthropic individuals followed suit with considerable donations.

The trustees assembled, organized, set to work. A philanthropic body, they drew from the like-minded far and near. Various agencies worked toward getting together and sifting the colonists for Georgia. Men visited the prisons for debtors and others. They did not choose at random, but when they found the truly unfortunate and undepraved in prison they drew them forth, compounded with their creditors, set the prisoners free, and enrolled them among the emigrants. Likewise they drew together those who, from sheer poverty, welcomed this opportunity. And they began a correspondence with distressed Protestants on the Continent. They also devised and used all manner of safeguards against imposition and the inclusion of any who would be wholly burdens, moral or physical. So it happened that, though misfortune had laid on almost all a heavy hand, the early colonists to Georgia were by no means undesirable flotsam and jetsam. The plans for the colony, the hopes for its well-being, wear a tranquil and fair countenance.

Oglethorpe himself would go with the first colonists. His ship was the *Anne* of two hundred tons burden — the last English colonizing ship with which this narrative has to do — and to her weathered sails there still clings a fascination. On board the *Anne*, beside the crew and master, are

Oglethorpe himself and more than a hundred and twenty Georgia settlers, men, women, and children. The *Anne* shook forth her sails in mid-November, 1732, upon the old West Indies sea road, and after two months of prosperous faring, came to anchor in Charles Town harbor.

South Carolina, approving this Georgia settlement which was to open the country southward and be a wall against Spain, received the colonists with hospitality. Oglethorpe and the weary colonists rested from long travel, then hoisted sail again and proceeded on their way to Port Royal, and southward yet to the mouth of the Savannah. Here there was further tarrying while Oglethorpe and picked men went in a small boat up the river to choose the site where they should build their town.

Here, upon the lower reaches, there lay a fair plateau, a mile long, rising forty feet above the stream. Near by stood a village of well-inclined Indians — the Yamacraws. Ships might float upon the river, close beneath the tree-crowned bluff. It was springtime now and beautiful in the southern land — the sky azure, the air delicate, the earth garbed in flowers. Little wonder then that Oglethorpe chose Yamacraw Bluff for his town.

A trader from Carolina was found here, and the trader's wife, a half-breed, Mary Musgrove by name, did the English good service. She made her Indian kindred friends with the newcomers. From the first Oglethorpe dealt wisely with the red men. In return for many coveted goods, he procured within the year a formal cession of the land between the two rivers and the islands off the coast. He swore friendship and promised to treat the Indians justly, and he kept his oath. The site chosen, he now returned to the *Anne* and presently brought his colonists up the river to that fair place. As soon as they landed, these first Georgians began immediately to build a town which they named Savannah.

Ere long other emigrants arrived. In 1734 came seventy-eight German Protestants from Salzburg, with Baron von Reck and two pastors for leaders. The next year saw fifty-seven others added to these. Then came Moravians with their pastor. All these strong, industrious, religious folk made settlements upon the river above Savannah. Italians came, Piedmontese sent by the trustees to teach the coveted silk-culture. Oglethorpe, when he sailed to England in 1734, took with him Tomochi-chi, chief of the Yamacraws, and other Indians.

English interest in Georgia increased. Parliament gave more money — £26,000. Oglethorpe and the trustees gathered more colonists. The Spanish cloud seemed to be rolling up in the south, and it was desirable to have in Georgia a number of men who were by inheritance used to war. Scotch Highlanders — there would be the right folk! No sooner said than gathered. Something under two hundred, courageous and hardy, were enrolled from the Highlands. The majority were men, but there were fifty women and children with them. All went to Georgia, where they settled to the south of Savannah, on the Altamaha, near the island of St. Simon. Other Highlanders followed. They had a fort and a town which they named New Inverness, and the region that they peopled they called Darien.

Oglethorpe himself left England late in 1735, with two ships, the *Symond* and the *London Merchant*, and several hundred colonists aboard. Of these folk doubtless a number were of the type the whole enterprise had been planned to benefit. Others were Protestants from the Continent. Yet others — notably Sir Francis Bathurst and his family — went at their own charges. After Oglethorpe himself, most remarkable perhaps of those going to Georgia were the brothers John and

Charles Wesley. Not precisely colonists are the
Wesleys, but prospectors for the souls of the colo-
nists, and the souls of the Indians — Yamacraws,
Uchees, and Creeks.

They all landed at Savannah, and now planned
to make a settlement south of their capital city,
by the mouth of Altamaha. Oglethorpe chose St.
Simon's Island, and here they built, and called
their town Frederica.

Each Freeholder had 60 Feet in Front by 90 Feet in
depth upon the high Street for House and Garden;
but those which fronted the River had but 30 in Front,
by 60 Feet in depth. Each Family had a Bower of
Palmetto Leaves finished upon the back Street in
their own Lands. The side toward the front Street
was set out for their Houses. These Palmetto Bowers
were very convenient shelters, being tight in the
hardest Rains; they were about 20 Feet long and 14
Feet wide, and in regular Rows looked very pretty,
the Palmetto Leaves lying smooth and handsome, and
of a good Colour. The whole appeared something
like a Camp; for the Bowers looked like Tents, only
being larger and covered with Palmetto Leaves.[1]

Their life sounds idyllic, but it will not always be
so. Thunders will arise; serpents be found in Eden.

[1] Moore's *Voyage to Georgia*. Quoted in Winsor's *Narrative and
Critical History of America*, vol. v, p. 378.

But here now we leave them — in infant Savan‧
nah — in the Salzburgers' village of Ebenezer and
in the Moravian village nearby — in Darien of
the Highlanders — and in Frederica, where until
houses are built they will live in palmetto bowers.

Virginia, Maryland, the two Carolinas, Georgia
— the southern sweep of England-in-America —
are colonized.   They have communication with
one another and with middle and northern England-in-America.   They also have communication
with the motherland over the sea.   The greetings
of kindred and the fruits of labor travel to and fro
over the salt, tumbling waves.   But also go mutu-
al criticism and complaint.   "Each man," says
Goethe, "is led and misled after a fashion peculiar
to himself."   So with those mass persons called
countries.   Tension would come about, tension
would relax, tension would return and increase
between Mother England and Daughter America.
In all these colonies, in the year with which this
narrative closes, there were living children and
young persons who would see the cord between
broken, would hear read the Declaration of Independence.   So — but the true bond could never be
broken, for mother and daughter after all are one

THE NAVIGATION LAWS

THREE acts of Parliament — the Navigation Act of 1660, the Staple Act of 1663, and the Act of 1673 imposing Plantation Duties — laid the foundation of the old colonial system of Great Britain. Contrary to the somewhat passionate contentions of older historians, they were not designed in any tyrannical spirit, though they embodied a theory of colonization and trade which has long since been discarded. In the seventeenth century colonies were regarded as plantations existing solely for the benefit of the mother country. Therefore their trade and industry must be regulated so as to contribute most to the sea power, the commerce, and the industry of the home country which gave them protection. Sir Josiah Child was only expressing a commonplace observation of the mercantilists when he wrote "That all colonies or plantations do endamage their Mother-Kingdoms, whereof the trades of such Plantations are not confined by severe Laws, and good execution of those Laws, to the Mother-Kingdom."

The Navigation Act of 1660, following the policy laid down in the statute of 1651 enacted under the Commonwealth, was a direct blow aimed at the Dutch, who were fast monopolizing the carrying trade. It forbade any goods to be imported into or exported from His Majesty's plantations except in English, Irish, or colonial vessels of which the master and three fourths of the crew must be English; and it forbade the importation into England of any goods produced in the plantations unless carried in English bottoms. Contemporary Englishmen hailed this act as the Magna Charta of the Sea. There was no attempt to disguise its purpose. "The Bent and Design," wrote Charles Davenant, "was to make those colonies as much dependant as possible upon their Mother-Country," by preventing them from trading independently and so diverting their wealth. The effect would be to give English, Irish, and colonial shipping a monopoly of the carrying trade within the Empire. The act also aided English merchants by the requirement that goods of foreign origin should be imported directly from the place of production; and that certain enumerated commodities of the plantations should be carried only to English ports. These enumerated commodities were products of the southern and semitropical plantations. "Sugars, Tobacco, Cotton-wool, Indicoes, Ginger, Fustick or other dyeing wood."

To benefit British merchants still more directly by making England the staple not only of plantation products but also of all commodities of all countries, the Act of 1663 was passed by Parliament. "No Commoditie of the Growth Production or Manufacture of Europe shall be imported into any Land Island Plantation Colony Territory or Place to His Majestie belonging . . . but what shall be bona fide and without fraude laden and shipped in England Wales [and] the Towne of Berwicke upon Tweede and in English built Shipping." The preamble to this famous act breathed no hostile intent. The design was to maintain "a greater correspondence and kindnesse" between the plantations and the mother country; to encourage shipping; to render navigation cheaper and safer; to make "this Kingdome a Staple not only of the Commodities of those Plantations but also of the Commodities of other Countries and places for the supplying of them" — it "being the usage of other nations to keepe their [Plantations] Trade to themselves."

The Act of 1673 was passed to meet certain difficulties which arose in the administration of the Act of 1660. The earlier act permitted colonial vessels to carry enumerated commodities from the place of production to another plantation without paying duties. Under cover of this provision, it was assumed that enumerated commodities, after being taken to a plantation, could then be sent directly to continental ports free of duty. The new act provided that, before vessels left a colonial port, bonds should be given that the enumerated commodities would be carried only to England. If bonds were not given and the commodities were taken to another colonial port, plantation duties were collected according to a prescribed schedule.

These acts were not rigorously enforced until after the passage of the administrative act of 1696 and the establishment of admiralty courts. Even then it does not appear that they bore heavily on the colonies, or occasioned serious protest. The trade acts of 1764 and 1765 are described in *The Eve of the Revolution.*— EDITOR.

BIBLIOGRAPHICAL NOTE

THE literature of the Colonial South is like the leaves of Vallombrosa for multitude. Here may be indicated some volumes useful in any general survey.

VIRGINIA

Hakluyt's *Principal Voyages*. 12 vols. (Hakluyt Society. Extra Series, 1905–1907.) "The Prose Epic of the modern English nation."

Purchas, His Pilgrims. 20 vols. (Hakluyt Society, Extra Series, 1905–1907.)

Hening's *Statutes at Large*, published in 1823, is an eminently valuable collection of the laws of colonial Virginia, beginning with the Assembly of 1619. Hening's own quotation from Priestley, "The Laws of a country are necessarily connected with everything belonging to the people of it: so that a thorough knowledge of them and of their progress would inform us of everything that was most useful to be known," indicates the range and weight of his thirteen volumes.

William Stith's *The History of the Discovery and First Settlement of Virginia* (1747) gives some valuable documents and a picture of the first years at Jamestown.

Alexander Brown's *Genesis of the United States*, 2 vols. (1890), is a very valuable work, giving historical manuscripts and tracts. Less valuable is his *First Re-public in America* (1898), in which the author attempts to weave his material into an historical narrative.

Philip A. Bruce's *Economic History of Virginia in the Seventeenth Century*, 2 vols. (1896), is a highly interest-ing and exhaustive survey. The same author has written *Social Life of Virginia in the Seventeenth Century* (1907) and *Institutional History of Virginia in the Seventeenth Century*, 2 vols. (1910).

John Fiske's *Virginia and Her Neighbors*, 2 vols. (1897), and John E. Cooke's *Virginia* (*American Com-monwealth Series*, 1883) are written in lighter vein than the foregoing histories and possess much literary dis-tinction.

On Captain John Smith there are writings innumer-able. Some writers give credence to Smith's own narra-tives, while others do not. John Fiske accepts the narra-tives as history, and Edward Arber, who has edited them (2 vols., 1884), holds that the *General History* (1624) is more reliable than the *True Relation* (1608). On the other side, as doubters of Smith's credibility, are ranged such weighty authorities as Charles Deane, Henry Adams, and Alexander Brown.

Thomas J. Wertenbaker's *Virginia under the Stuarts* (1914) is a painstaking effort to set forth the political history of the colony in the light of recent historical investigation, but the book is devoid of literary at-tractiveness.

MARYLAND

The Archives of Maryland, 37 vols. (1883–) contain the official documents of the province.

John L. Bozman's *History of Maryland*, 2 vols. (1837), contains much valuable material for the years 1634–1658.

J. T. Scharf's *History of Maryland*, 3 vols. (1879), is a solid piece of work; but the reader will turn by preference to the more readable books by John Fiske, *Virginia and Her Neighbors*, and William H. Browne, *Maryland, The History of a Palatinate* (*American Commonwealth Series*, 1884). Browne has also written *George and Cecilius Calvert* (1890).

THE CAROLINAS

The Colonial Records of North Carolina, 10 vols. (1886–1890), are a mine of information about both North and South Carolina.

Francis L. Hawks's *History of North Carolina*, 2 vols. (1857-8), remains the most substantial work on the colony to the year 1729.

Samuel A. Ashe's *History of North Carolina* (1908) carries the political history down to 1783.

Edward McCrady's *History of South Carolina under the Proprietary Government* (1897) and *South Carolina under the Royal Government* (1899) have superseded the older histories by Ramsay and Hewitt.

GEORGIA

The best histories of Georgia are those by William B. Stevens, 2 vols. (1847, 1859), and Charles C. Jones, 2 vols. (1883). Robert Wright's *Memoir of General James Oglethorpe* (1867) is still the best life of the founder of Georgia.

In the *American Nation Series* and in Winsor's *Narrative and Critical History of America,* the reader will find accounts of the Southern colonies written by specialists and accompanied by much critical apparatus.   Further lists will be found appended to the articles on the several States in *The Encyclopædia Britannica,* 11th edition.

INDEX